A

FINLEY

FAMILY HISTORY

By

J. Wayne Johnson, MD

First published by AuthorHouse 06/07/04

ISBN: 1-4184-8037-1 (e-book)
ISBN: 1-4184-1538-3 (Paperback)
ISBN: 1-4184-1539-1 (Dust Jacket)

Library of Congress Control Number: 2003098576

Printed in the United States of America
Bloomington, IN

This book is printed on acid free paper.

INTRODUCTION

This book is the result of research I have done to trace my Finley ancestors. Many have helped along the way. In the early days, Dr. Carmen J. Finley and James Finley were valuable correspondents. Among many things, Carmen first called my attention to a power of attorney document in Madison County, Kentucky deeds that proved eventually to be the key to understanding the first couple of generations of my ancestors. Virginia Hunt provided information of Georgia Indian Depredation Records that showed that our Greene County, Georgia Finleys were the sons of George Finley I. Until I received those records, I had thought that they were the sons of James Finley of Mecklenburg County, North Carolina. Many others have contributed facts helping understand family relationships.

The line as presented in this book is based on facts discovered in research. Unfortunately, is some cases the facts are sketchy and several times I have had to change relationships as new facts became available. Reconstructing the family line is similar to working a puzzle in which many of the pieces of the puzzle are missing. There is one linkage I have not been able to support as well as desired. I spent several years' effort on nothing else but compiling as much information as I could find on William Finley I (c1783-1840) and George Finley II (c1755-1835). I feel certain George was the father of William, but I have not been able to prove it without a trace of doubt. George owned little property during his lifetime and thus few records are available. The only record I could find about his death was an item in Newton County, Georgia records that Zachariah Finley was appointed the administrator of his estate in January, 1836. There is no record of the names of his children and so it is impossible to prove he even had a son named William. Censuses of Georgia from 1790 to 1820 had been destroyed by the English when they sacked Washington in the War of 1812, so we do not even have an indication of how many children George II had or their approximate ages. Even so, there is much circumstantial evidence that George II was the father of William I. Despairing of ever proving it, I have decided to present this as a fact. I certainly welcome anyone sending me information they may have found that either proves or disproves the relationship. The same applies for any other relationship as presented in this book. One thing that a genealogist learns is that facts sometime appear from unsuspected sources that change one's opinions.

This difficulty connecting William Finley to George Finley II made it necessary to search for all the information I could find on all the Finleys living near William in Georgia. In most cases, I could rule out most of them as William's father. I came to possess information on many other Finleys not related to my line. I have recorded this information in Chapter 13, entitled "Finleys of Early Piedmont, Georgia." Hopefully, this information will assist others to trace their own ancestry.

I can see only three possibilities as to the father of William Finley I. One is that he was the son of George II as presented in this book. The other is that there was another Finley family in which the father died shortly after moving to Georgia before buying land and thus leaving no record of his presence. I believe this is unlikely. The third possibility is Amon Finley of Greene County, Georgia (# 18 in Chapter 13). He had two draws in the 1805 Land Lottery, so he had at least one child in 1803. Unfortunately, I have no other information on him. There is no reason to believe William I is his son. I also believe it is unlikely that William was the son of a Finley of a nearby state, such as South or North Carolina. If I am right that Nicholas Finley, Samuel Finley, and Thomas Finley II of early Clarke County, Georgia were his brothers, then there is no Finley family in either of those states in the 1790 or 1800 censuses who had enough sons to qualify as possible candidates as the ancestors of these Clarke County brothers.

It was common practice in early days for a man to name his first son after his wife's father, the second son for his father, and succeeding sons for each of his brothers. This led to many Finleys with the same given names. In this book, I have arbitrarily given Finleys with the same first name Roman Numerals after their names to differentiate them from each other. I have not given designations of senior or junior in this book, even though father and son may have the same name. This use of the terms is of rather modern invention. In early days, the terms were used to differentiate any two men living in the same community having the same names. They could have been father-son, uncle-nephew, or not related in any way. This means that George Finley II might have been known as George Finley Jr. while his father was alive, but as George Finley Sr. when his son became grown.

Most of the names in early documents were spelled phonetically. Most of the documents were also written by someone else, not the person himself. Thus the same man's name was often spelled differently in different documents. Sometimes it was even spelled differently in different places in the same document. Thus the name Finley was variously spelled Findley, Finlay, Findlay and many other variants. Some descendants of the a family spelled the name differently from other descendants of the same family. When people became better educated, the spelling became more consistent, but not so in early times. The spelling in this book is generally Finley, since that is the way my own family spells it.

Our Finley ancestors appear to prove the statement that has been made about the Scotch-Irish in general - that they were restless and frequently moved about. George Finley I moved the farthest, from Scotland to this country. He probably lived first in Pennsylvania before he moved to Mecklenburg County, North Carolina. He then moved again to Greene County, Georgia shortly before his death. Succeeding generations lived in several different counties in Georgia and Alabama. Some of their siblings moved even farther, mostly to the West. In almost no case can their descendants be found still living in the counties where they lived in the early days.

In frontier times, counties were often organized containing vast amounts of territory. As they became more thickly settled, they were often divided into several additional counties. Thus it was common for a man to buy land in one county, but the same land was in another county when he sold it. The purchase was recorded in the records of the first county, but the sale of the same land was recorded in the records of the second county. For instance, our Finley ancestors bought land in Mecklenburg County, North Carolina but some of the same land is now in Cabarrus County and some in Union County. In situations like this, this book records that they lived in Mecklenburg County with the current name of the county following in parentheses.

Finding this information has provided me with countless hours of pleasure. I only hope this book will provide just a fraction of as much pleasure to others.

Sarah Fulton provided the information on the descendants of Nicholas Finley; Virginia Hunt on descendants of George Finley III; Dr. Wayne

Finley on descendants of Augustus Clay Finley;
Elvie Hayes on descendants of Augustus Bernard
Finley; Willis T. Finley on those of Eleven
Finley; Jan Burford on those of Robert Finley
III; Lleta Lightfoot on those of Norris
Finley; Libba Woodall on those of James Finley
III; Annie Lucille Walthall those of Charles
Lee Finley; and many others helped in many
ways to untangle relationships.

THE CLASSIFICATION SYSTEM

The original immigrant to this country of this family, George Finley I, is given the number 0, which does not appear in the text. His sons are given one digit as their number. Wherever known, they are numbered in the order of their birth. The next generation of sons is given the same digit as their father, with a second digit added, numbered again in the order of their birth. One can tell at a glance how many generations a person is removed from the original immigrant by the number of digits in his classification number. Thus William E. Finley, #33172, is five generations removed from George Finley I. He is the second son of #3317, James Taylor Finley. James is the seventh son of #331, Augustus H. Finley, and so on. This system breaks down in families having more than 10 children, not uncommon in early generations. For this reason, females are not given a number of their own, but are given their next older brother's number followed by a decimal and then a number. There is no suggestion intended that they were less important in the family.

Abbreviations

a	=	after
b	=	by or before
c	=	circa
bur	=	buried at
d	=	daughter of
dy	=	died young
m	=	married
ni	=	no issue
nm	=	never married
s	=	son of
DB	=	Deed Book
WB	=	Will Book
?	=	probably

TABLE OF CONTENTS

Chapter 1

HISTORY OF THE CLAN FINLEY

I remember asking my grandfather, Will Finley, if he knew where his ancestors originated. He replied that they were Scotch-Irish. I thought at the time he meant a group of Scotsmen and a group of Irishmen intermarried and their children were Scotch-Irish. As I have become interested in the family history I have found this is not the meaning of the term at all. The Scotch-Irish were a group of Scots who immigrated to Northern Ireland in the 17th century and after a period of time immigrated again to America. Since they were Scots who moved to this country from Ireland, they eventually became known as Scotch-Irish. In the case of our Finley ancestors, it appears they came to this country directly from Scotland, but they lived among the Scotch-Irish so they essentially were a part of that group.

All Finleys, Fenleys, Findleys, Finlays and other variations of the spelling can trace

their name to the Clan Finley of Scotland, the
only place of origin for the name. The Clan
Finley or Fionnladh (early spelling) was a
sept of the Clan Farquharson (pronounced
Fark'-a-son), who inhabited the highland area
of Moray Province. The Queen's castle,
Balmoral, is located on the edge of their
territory. One of the explanations of the
origin of the name relates that one of the
outstanding warriors of the Clan Farquharson
was named Finley and his descendants
thereafter used this as their surname. The
name Finley is a contraction of the Gaelic
words fionn meaning white or blond and ladh
meaning warrior. Thus the usual meaning of
the name is given as blond warrior.

Many Finleys claim their lineage traces beyond
the Clan Farquharson to MacBheatha or MacBeth,
king of Scotland from 1040 to 1057, he being
chief of the Clan Finley before becoming king.
While I have not been able to prove this claim
in my reading, history does reveal many facts
suggesting they may be right. MacBeth was the
son of Findlaech (Findley) Mac Ruaridh
(MacCrory), thane of Ross and Cromarty and
later mormaer (earl) of Moray. Stout says
Findley was a lineal descendant of Lorne, the
first king of Scotland. (After his death,
Lorne was succeeded as king by his younger
brother, Fergus. Thereafter the line of kings
of Scotland came from the descendants of
Fergus.) MacBeth was also a descendent of
Fergus through his mother.

Findley married Donada, daughter of Malcolm
II, king of Scotland from 1005 to 1034.
Malcolm had no sons but three daughters. Thus
MacBeth was the grandson of the king and had a

legitimate claim to the throne. After Malcolm's death, Duncan, cousin of MacBeth and also a grandson of Malcolm, was crowned king.

Shakespeare immortalized MacBeth but maligned him in the process. He based his play on a tradition current in his time but since proved in error. He probably was also influenced by his patron, King James I of England (James VI of Scotland) who was a descendant of Duncan. King James considered himself an authority on witchcraft. He had written a book on the subject in his youth and it was probably through his influence that the witches' scenes were included in the play.

According to Shakespeare, MacBeth killed Duncan in his bed while Duncan was a guest in MacBeth's castle. History tells a different story. It seems Duncan tried to consolidate his power by eliminating his chief rivals. He invaded Moray and Caithness to subdue or eliminate MacBeth and Thorfinn (another grandson of Malcolm II and thus also a claimant to the throne). In defending his homeland, MacBeth slew Duncan in the ensuing battle, not in his bed. Thereafter, MacBeth was crowned King of Scotland. MacBeth became more popular than Duncan and is generally considered an outstanding king of Scotland.

MacBeth had married Gruoch, widow of his cousin Gilcomgain and granddaughter of Kenneth II, king prior to Malcolm II. Some say her son Lulach, stepson of MacBeth, had the strongest claim to the throne. To understand the situation, one must consider that the succession of Scottish kings was by the law of tanistry.

The succession of kings in England was by the law of primo-geniture but not so at the time in Scotland. In Scotland the tanist or strongest member of the royal family became king. Thus MacBeth, as the tanist of his infant stepson, became king. The fact that MacBeth was a legitimate king of Scotland is born out by his burial on the island of Iona, traditionally the burial place of true kings of Scotland, but not of usurpers.

St. Berchan, a contemporary of MacBeth, said of him, "The strong one was fair, yellow haired and tall. Very pleasant was the handsome youth to me. Brimful of food was Scotland, east and west, during the reign of the ruddy, brave king." He proved to be an outstanding king, establishing systematic courts of justice. He was a benefactor of the church. In 1050, he made a pilgrimage to Rome where it is said he "scattered money among the poor like seed." He was slain in a battle at Lumphanan in Aberdeenshire in 1057 by followers of Malcolm Canmore (Malcolm III), son of Duncan.

Peter Ellis says this of MacBeth, "To talk of Shakespeare's Macbeth as the MacBeth of historical reality is, indeed, to malign a ruler who stands head and shoulders above the feuds and petty squabbles which ravaged the kingdoms of Europe in the eleventh century. It is ironic that MacBeth and Scotland were singled out by Shakespeare when the contemporary dynastic struggles in England were, by comparison, far more murderous. While rulers came and went in neighbouring England, Norway and Denmark, MacBeth ruled in security and peace in Scotland. At no time during MacBeth's kingship did a Scottish army march outside the borders of Scotland, and for the first fourteen years of his reign no envious monarch in England, Norway or Denmark felt strong enough to invade Scottish territory. MacBeth brought peace and security to Scotland. Elsewhere the great royal families of Europe demonstrated how efficiently they could kill, cheat and rob. One English monarch had his brother's eyes put out for attempting to claim the throne, another had his brother's body dug up and beheaded. Poisoners practiced their skills freely, as brothers and cousins, even mothers and sons, turned on each other in a bloody scramble for power."

MacBeth is considered the last great Celtic king of Scotland. He along with his predecessors were elected Ard Righ, or High King, by the Mormaers, or provincial rulers of Scotland. He and his predecessors ruled by the right of Tanistry. The Scottish Church was independent of the Roman Church. After short reigns by Lulach and Donald Ban, Malcolm Canmore ruled for many years. He was succeeded by four of his sons in succession, the family ruling for many years. After their reigns, kings were thereafter crowned by right of primogeniture, as in England. David, the youngest son of Malcolm Canmore, grew up in the English court, and brought many of his friends, who were Normans, and established them as earls in Scotland. Scottish society in the lowlands became feudal, as it was in England, as contrasted with the clan system, which still prevailed in the Highlands. Malcolm Canmore married Margaret, the daughter of the former king of England, who was a devout Roman Catholic. Under her influence, Roman Catholic priests were introduced into Scotland and the Church of Scotland eventually became part of the Roman Church.

Stout hints that for protection from their enemies (Malcolm Canmore and his sons who succeeded him as king), Macbeth's descendants moved to the highlands of Moray and assumed the name Farquharson. After several generations some of them resumed using the name Finley. It seems reasonable that a family fearing the king (Malcolm Canmore proved to be a vengeful and unscrupulous king) would move to the nearest mountainous area for protection, where the Clan Farquharson settled, and there is no doubt MacBeth was the son of a man named Finley.

Most of the Finleys gradually migrated from the highlands to Angus and Fife and especially to Glasgow and its environs by the seventeenth century. Most of them along with their lowlander neighbors converted to Presbyterianism during the Protestant Reformation.

One of the interesting legends concerning the Clan Farquharson concerns their call to arms. In times of danger, clansmen bearing fiery crosses rallied the clan for battle. They called the name of the meeting-place, "Carn-ne-cuimhne," now known as Cairnaquheen. Each clansman brought a stone and placed it on a pile. Those who survived the ensuing battle retrieved their stones and carried them home. Thus the remaining stones became a memorial for those who did not return. This

Farquharson cairn of remembrance is today enclosed by a fence on the south side of the Aberdeen to Braemar road between the 51st and 52nd milestones.

Chapter 2

HISTORY OF THE SCOTS AND THE SCOTCH-IRISH

According to tradition, the Scots derived their name from Scota, daughter of a Pharaoh of Egypt. She married Milesius, a descendant of Phenius, king of the Scythians. They settled on the Bay of Biscay, apparently in Northern Spain. Four of their sons, Heber, Heremon, Ith, and Ir invaded Ireland with a fleet of 30 ships and conquered the land.

A tribe known as the Scots or Scotti descended from Heremon. They established the kingdom of Dalriada in what is now County Antrim of Northern Ireland. In the 5th century AD, Erc, king of Dalriada, invaded the northern portion of Great Britain and established a successful colony of the Scots in Argyl. Lorne, his oldest son, became the first Melisian king of what is now Scotland. A second son, Angus McErc, held fief of Islay and other regions. After the death of Lorne, Fergus McErc, the youngest son, became king and consolidated the kingdom. It was from the sons of Fergus that the royal line of kings developed in Scotland. It is said Fergus was killed in a boating accident near the shore of Ireland on one of his trips back. The location is now named Carrickfergus, or Rock of Fergus. Carrickfergus is located near Belfast.

Over the next few centuries, the kingdom of Dalriada in Northern Ireland diminished and disappeared from history with the invasion of the Normans, but the kingdom became stronger in the northern portion of Great Britain. There they had constant warfare with the Picts, the original inhabitants. Kenneth McAlpin, king of the Scots in the ninth century, married the daughter of the king of the Picts, thus establishing control of the entire northern part of the island and giving it its present name of Scotland.

In the late seventeenth century Queen Elizabeth carried out a scorched earth policy in Northern Ireland, dispossessing many of the Catholics of their land. Her successor, James VI of Scotland and James I of England, opened this land for settlement by Scots. Great numbers of the lowlanders moved and prospered in Ulster. They were especially noted for their wool and later linen manufacturing.

They continued to have constant warfare with their Irish Catholic neighbors, who understandably felt that the land rightfully belonged to them. This conflict between the Catholics and Protestants in Northern Ireland has continued to the present day. After a few generations, the English wool merchants became jealous of their more prosperous Scot competitors and they persuaded the English Parliament to pass restrictive trade laws. These laws destroyed the woolen trade in Northern Ireland. Religious persecution also began to be applied with the Test Acts. Under these acts no one could hold public office unless he took communion in the Anglican Church.

In the beginning of the eighteenth century, many Presbyterians were dispossessed of their lands. This came through what was called the Rack-Renting system. In Northern Ireland, the Scotch-Irish rented their land for long periods of time, 30-40 years or more. Many of these leases began to expire in the early eighteenth century and the English overlords doubled or tripled the rents. The culmination of all these factors motivated many of the Scotch-Irish to emigrate to America.

The earliest emigration of the Scotch-Irish was to Maryland in about 1685. Over the next few decades the center of their migration was to the Eastern Shore of the Chesapeake Bay. By about 1717, they had settled all the Eastern Shore up to Cecil County, Maryland and were filling Southeastern Pennsylvania as well. Thereafter Pennsylvania became the principal first stop for the Scotch-Irish migrants. It is estimated that as many as one quarter million people emigrated from Northern Ireland between 1715 and 1775. This made them the largest homogeneous group of immigrants to this country at the time of the Revolution. Their long conflicts with the English led them to have little respect for the English crown. In fact, they had very little respect for central government of any kind. They had been fighting the English for their freedom for hundreds of years. Their move to Northern Ireland had loosened their feudal ties so they were fertile ground for the ideas of democracy. In their new country they became a potent force for liberty. During the Revolution they sided almost universally with the patriots. In addition they had been hardened by years of conflict and they made excellent soldiers. It is probable that without their contribution, the United States never would have won its independence from England.

These early Scots immigrants were almost all Presbyterians. They were frequently referred as Irishmen or Ulstermen, since that is where they lived immediately prior to immigration. They did not seem to mind at the time. However, when large numbers of Irish Catholics began to migrate to this country in the middle of the nineteenth century, they began to insist on being called Scotch-Irish to differentiate themselves from the Catholics.

By the middle of the eighteenth century the frontier areas of Virginia, North and South Carolina and Georgia were opening up. Land and taxes were cheaper than in Maryland and Pennsylvania. The Scotch-Irish streamed southward and settled the frontier areas of the South. The first area to be settled in this southern flood of migration was the Great Valley of Virginia. Next they settled in Rowan County, North Carolina, beginning about 1750. As succeeding waves of immigrants arrived, they settled Mecklenburg and surrounding counties and proceeded into South Carolina and eventually into Georgia. Thus

11

they contributed the largest gene pool for current inhabitants of the southern states.

The Scotch-Irish were troublesome settlers for the authorities. Pennsylvania Provincial Secretary James Logan wrote, "a settlement of five families from the North of Ireland gives me more trouble than fifty of any other people." For a time after 1729, he even refused to grant land to them. Their response to this was to increasingly settle on unoccupied land without official title. This was the beginning of a practice which became more and more common on the frontier - squatting. They came so swiftly that officials could not keep track of them. By the time they could survey the situation, the land had for so long been cultivated by squatters that they assumed they had established a right to it and resisted all efforts to expel them.

Leyburn says the "Scotch-Irish...were regarded as quick-tempered, impetuous, inclined to work by fits and starts, reckless, too much given to drinking. No contemporary observer praised them as model farmers. Their interest in politics on the Provincial level was soon to become active, even tempestuous; and their fame as Indian fighters was to become almost as notable as their reputation for causing trouble with the Indians."

Leyburn also says concerning the Revolution, the "Scotch-Irish support for independence was generally ardent. It showed itself in the actual fighting. There is wide agreement on the excellence of the soldiers who were Scotch-Irish. Wertenbaker says that they 'constituted the very back-bone of Washington's army. At Valley Forge, when many deserted him, they remained despite cold and hunger, to keep alive the waning cause.' Joseph Galloway claimed that half the army was Scotch-Irish. Ralph Barton Perry asserted that 'when account is taken of the Scotch-Irish Presbyterians, the Germans of the middle and southern colonies, and the New England congregationalists, it is safe to say that the bulk of the revolutionary armies came from dissenters of the reformed or Calvinistic sects. From the clergy of these sects came also the religious leadership.' A British major-general is reported to have testified before a committee of the House of Commons that 'half the rebel Continental Army were from Ireland'- that is, Scotch-Irish. General Howe indirectly paid tribute to the excellent marksmanship of the Scotch-Irish, learned as hunters and Indian fighters, and to their rifles 'perfected with little knowledge of ballistics.'"

Chapter 3

THE FINLEYS OF MECKLENBURG COUNTY, NORTH CAROLINA

The first place in which we can definitely locate our ancestor, George Finley I, is in Mecklenburg County, North Carolina. He first bought land there in 1773. In order to trace George Finley I beyond Mecklenburg County, North Carolina, we have carefully studied all the Finleys who seem to be related to him. The first to move into the area was Robert Finley who lived in Rowan County, North Carolina as early as 1762. He died sometime before 13 Jan 1763, when Alexander Cathey was appointed the administrator of his estate (Rowan Co. Court of Pleas and Quarter Sessions, 1763-1774, P. 1). Alexander Cathey was likely appointed administrator because no close relatives lived in the area at the time, and Cathey was likely the largest creditor of the estate.

From the Revolutionary War pension application of his son, Charles Finley (National Archives

S 6845), we know James Finley lived in Frederick County, Maryland in 1758 and that he moved to Mecklenburg County, North Carolina in 1763, probably in the fall after he had made his crop in Maryland. He settled on 12 Mile Creek in Mecklenburg (Union) County, North Carolina. On 14 January 1764, a James Finley was appointed to take the place of Alexander Cathey as administrator of the estate of Robert Finley of Rowan County. The timing of his move and the absence of any other Finleys in the area at the time convince us this was James Finley of 12 Mile Creek. James and Robert must have been related and probably were brothers. There is no mention of a widow or children of Robert Finley, so he was likely a bachelor.

James Finley of 12 Mile Creek died in 1806 and in his will he named five sons and five daughters. All his sons and all but one or two of his daughters had moved out of his house by the time the 1790 census was taken. We know from the pension application mentioned above that son Charles Finley was born in 1758. Censuses show that son William Finley and daughter Jannet Finley were born after 1760. Thus James seems to be a contemporary of our George Finley I (see Chapter 5).

John Finley and James Finley bought adjacent tracts of land on Rocky River in Mecklenburg (Cabarrus) County, North Carolina on the same day in 1769. Later we will explain why we think this is the same James Finley who lived on 12 Mile Creek. (Even if they were not the same, it would make no difference in the ancestry of George Finley I.) John Finley moved in 1784 to the North Fork of the Potomac

River in Virginia (West Virginia) and died there by 1785. John was the father of Rev. Robert Wilkes Finley whose birth date is usually given as 1750. From the Revolutionary War pension application of John's son, George (National Archives # W 7273), we know he had a son born in 1761. So John Finley was also a contemporary of George Finley I.

Let us pause to sum up our findings so far. Since James and John Finley bought adjacent tracts of land on the same day, they were undoubtedly closely related. Their children were near the same ages so they were contemporaries and very likely brothers. Robert Finley of Rowan County was likely another brother.

The next Finley appearing in Mecklenburg County was our George I who moved there by 1773. The land he bought on Caldwell Creek was adjacent to land belonging to a James Finley, probably the same James Finley mentioned above. His land was about 15 miles southeast of the land on Rocky River belonging to James and John Finley and about 25 miles northeast of the land on 12 Mile Creek belonging to James Finley. We have already noted that the children of George Finley I were near the same ages of those of James and John Finley. This likely means that he was a contemporary of Robert, John, and James. His close connection to Thomas Finley I (see below) convinces us that he was another brother.

Thomas Finley I bought from James Finley the land on Rocky River in 1777. This made him a next-door neighbor of John Finley. This suggests strongly that Thomas was related to James and John Finley. Thomas had moved to Wilkes (Oglethorpe) County, Georgia by 1785 and by 1790 he lived in Greene County, Georgia where he lived in the same tax district as George Finley I. (Mecklenburg Co. DB 13, p. 588 and Cabarrus Co. DB 2, p. 487 prove these moves.) When he applied for a land grant in Georgia, 100 acres of it was for the headrights of George Finley. His daughter Lucinda Finley married Robert I, the son of George Finley I. George's sons James and Robert I witnessed Thomas' will.

The oldest child of Thomas Finley I appears to be Jane, who married Charles Gillium in 1790, suggesting she was born around 1775. (Fifteen was about the average age of first marriage for girls at the time.) Some of the sons of George Finley I had children about the same ages as the children of Thomas. It seems that Thomas Finley was near the same age as the oldest sons of George Finley I. We might consider that Thomas I was a son of George Finley I except that his daughter married a son of George. It is not likely a man married his niece. It is likely that Thomas was the son of either James or John Finley. He is not mentioned in the will of James Finley, but that might be explained by the fact he died before James did. It is more likely he was the son of John. There has been no will or estate records found for John. The power of attorney document mentioned on the next page gives us the names of four of his sons but may not contain all of them. It appears only those living in Kentucky at the time signed the document. Thomas Finley I and Joseph Finley were living in Georgia then, which explains why they did not also sign it, assuming that they were also sons of John. (See pages 171-2 and 186-7 for more on Joseph Finley).

Chapter 4

POSSIBLE ORIGIN OF THE MECKLENBURG FINLEYS

The document which most likely will lead us to the ancestors of the Mecklenburg County Finleys is found in Madison County, Kentucky Deed Book D, pp. 63-4, dated before 2 Aug 1796. In it, John, Samuel, and Robert W. Finley, legatees of John Finley, deceased, gave power of attorney to George Finley to sell land on Rocky River in Cabarrus County, North Carolina. The deceased John Finley was obviously the John who had bought the land on Rocky River (when it was located in Mecklenburg County). In his Revolutionary War pension application (National Archives # W 7273), John Finley's son George reveals he served in Mecklenburg County, North Carolina, married in Madison County, Kentucky and lived in Lawrence County, Tennessee in 1832 at the time of his application. The most important thing for our search is that this power of attorney document shows us that the Rev.

Robert Wilkes Finley was the son of John Finley of Mecklenburg County.

Rev. Robert Wilkes Finley was born in 1750 in Bucks County, Pennsylvania. He was educated at Princeton College in New Jersey. One of his mentors there was Rev. John Witherspoon, president of the college and one of the signers of the Declaration of Independence. Robert W. Finley married Rebecca Bradley, the daughter of James Bradley, in 1780. James Bradley lived on Long Creek in Mecklenburg County, North Carolina at the time. Robert was pastor of the Waxhaw Presbyterian Church, which was located in Lancaster County, South Carolina about one or two miles from the Mecklenburg (Union) County line, from about 1784 to 1789. During this time, he also served as supply preacher for Providence Presbyterian Church and probably other churches of Mecklenburg County which were without pastors. About 1789 he moved to the area between the North and South Forks of the Potomac River in Virginia (West Virginia). Soon afterward he moved to Kentucky where he lived in Mason, Fleming, and Bourbon Counties. When he signed the power of attorney document, he lived in Bourbon County. In 1796, he moved to Ohio near where Chillicothe now is located.

Herald Stout says Rev. Robert Wilkes Finley was the grandson of Robert Finley of Glasgow and/or Paisley, Scotland (Stout's 2-40). This seems likely since Wilkes appears to be a family name and the elder Robert Finley married Catherine Wilkes. Stout lists sons of Robert and Catherine named Robert, James, John, and George, among others. (He says George died young, but it is certainly possible he was mistaken about this.) He says Rev. Robert Wilkes Finley was the son of James Finley, but records show he was the son of John instead. It is very likely that John, James, and George Finley I of Mecklenburg County and Robert Finley of Rowan County were the sons of Robert and Catherine Wilkes Finley of Paisley, Scotland.

In his autobiography, Rev. James Bradley Finley, son of Rev. Robert Wilkes Finley, gave two very important statements for our purposes. He said his "paternal grandfather (ie, John Finley of Mecklenburg County, North Carolina) was of the old stock of Pennsylvanians from Scotland." He also stated that his paternal grandfather, being a younger son of his father, received none of the inheritance, thus went "to the El Dorado of the western world (ie, America), in quest of his fortune." Rev. James B. Finley clearly suggested that John Finley came to this country from Scotland rather than from Ireland and that he came as an adult. These two facts allow us to rule out most of the Finleys we might otherwise consider the ancestors of the Mecklenburg County Finleys. It should be noted that most of the Finleys who immigrated to America came from Ireland rather than from Scotland. They, their fathers or grandfathers, had previously moved from Scotland to Northern Ireland.

Without these statements, we might give serious consideration to Archibald Finley as the father of our Mecklenburg County Finleys. He was an early immigrant to Bucks County, Pennsylvania, which was also the location of our John Finley when his son Robert Wilkes was born. Archibald Finley died on 11 Mar 1749/50. (The slash in the year reminds us that the secular and church calendars started the new year at different times. Archibald died in 1749 by the church calendar but in 1750 by the calendar we use today.) His will and estate papers show that Archibald's eldest son was named John. Son Henry was also old enough to serve as coadministrator. The will was witnessed by a James Finley, who might be another son old enough to witness the will. Alexander Finley, son of Archibald, bought land in 1749 (see Bucks Co. DB 24, p. 286). A young man had to be at least eighteen years of age to purchase land and most were older before buying their first land. Thus Archibald Finley had three or four sons born before 1731. The next son we can identify as his is Archibald (Jr.) who according to military records was born in 1738. We thus know Archibald had a son named John old enough to be the John Finley of Mecklenburg County, North Carolina, and possibly a son named James. There is a big enough gap in the births of Alexander and Archibald Jr. that he could have had several other sons. However, Archibald immigrated to this country from County Armagh, Ireland. Moreover, none of his sons came to this country as adults. In addition, it is generally accepted that his son John is the John Finley who married Elizabeth Harris. This John is credited with leading Daniel Boone into Kentucky through the Cumberland Gap. We can rule Archibald out as the father of our Mecklenburg County Finleys.

Herald Stout says Michael Finley, brother of Archibald Finley, first lived in Bucks County when he came to this country. It is well documented that Michael's son, Rev. Samuel Finley, attended Tennent's Log College, which was located in Bucks County. Rev. Samuel Finley was president of Princeton College from 1760 to 1765. He was the great grandfather of Samuel Finley Breese Morse, the inventor of the telegraph. Because of the prominence of Rev. Samuel Finley, the family of Michael Finley is well known. Without belaboring the point more, we can be sure Michael is not the father of our Mecklenburg County Finleys.

There is evidence that Thomas Allison, who died in London Brittain township of Chester County, Pennsylvania in 1738, was the father in law of James Finley of 12 Mile Creek in Mecklenburg County, North Carolina (see Chapter 12). A neighbor of his was Charles Finley who was taxed in London Brittain township from 1725 to 1740. Charles probably had a son named John who was first taxed in the same township in 1734. Both Charles and John Finley witnessed the will of Roger Evans in 1738/9 (Chester Co., PA WB 1, p. 167), so Charles and John Finley probably were father and son. Nothing is known of the whereabouts of Charles Finley after 1740. He certainly could have had more children. He could have moved to Bucks County for all we know. There is nothing to suggest it, but extant records of Bucks County before the 1760's are very scarce. He could have lived in Bucks and there might be no evidence of it. However, we can rule him out as the ancestor of our Mecklenburg County Finleys if the statements of Rev. James Bradley Finley are correct. We do not know if Charles Finley immigrated from Scotland or from Ireland, but we can be sure his children did not come as adults.

The following genealogy of our ancestors when they lived in Scotland and their migrations is taken almost entirely from Herald Stout's book, <u>The Clan Finley</u>. I have made no attempt to verify it. (I basically have copied his work, but am not using quotation marks since I have added and rearranged some words and phrases to provide a more narrative account. I have also used words in some places where he used symbols.) Stout's work seems to be based on earlier research done by Albert Finley France. France was the librarian of the Naval Academy around 1925 when he did his research.

1. Fearchar McFinlay who married _____ MacDonachadh, was the fourth son of Shaw Dubh, Chief of Clan Fionnladh or Finlay, a sept of Clan Chattan. In 1236 he held large tracts at Strathdie, Parish of Crothie, in the Braces of Mar at the head of Aberdeenshire, Scotland. His large family of sons adopted variants of the Clan names such as McFarchar, Farquharson, McFinlay, etc. They settled on the borders of Perth and Angus. His second son was:

2. Archibald Finlay (-b1337) who married Margaret Robertson, daughter of William Robertson of Lude. He distinguished himself at the Battle of Largs, 21 October 1263, between the Scots and the Norwegians. In 1314 he was mentioned in a charter as occupying ½ marcate of land at Rousknot, Perthshire. He was the father of:

3. William Finlay who married Isabell Dempster, daughter of the Laird of Murisk, Thomas Dempster and Eleanor Forbes, co-heir of Viscount Forbes. William was a tenant and

forester of King Robert I at Rousknot, Perthshire. He was the father of:

4. Andrew Finlay who married Margorie McDonald, niece and co-heir of John McDonald of Perth. Andrew was a portioner of Menmur and sheriff of Perth. In 1379 he was granted amercements by Robert II as fees. He was the father of:

5. John Finlay (1356-?1456) who married Elinor Stewart, daughter of John Stewart of Fothergill. In 1406, John Finley was bishop of Dumblain, Perthshire. His title was Reginald of the Isles, Thane of Glentilt, being 3 devaches of land. In 1425, he was tutor of James, son of Murdock, Duke of St. Albans. He was the father of:

6. John Finlay (-1461) who married Mary McRae (-a1462). In 1457 he transferred 17 townships of Thanage of Glentilt to son John. He served as heir to his father John le Thane in the lands of Pepnocrife in Strathquay, later sold. In 1457-61 he lived near Cupar Angus Cistercian Abbey, Kethyl Twp., Forfashire, leasing one-twelfth of Cupar Grange. He was the father of:

7. John Finlay (-a1507) who married Janet Roger, daughter of William Roger of Cupar Angus. In 1463 he held one-sixth of Combryeland at Pentecoast, Forfashire and leased one-twelfth of Cupar Grange. He was the father of:

8. Andrew Finley (-1546) who married in 1523 Janet Hay, daughter of John and Janet (Douglas) Hay of Erroll, Perthshire;

descendant of David de Haya, sheriff of Forfashire and of William de la Haya, Cup Bearer to Malcolm IV. Andrew occupied one-fourth portion of Aughinleyth at Pentecoast up to 1546. In 1507, he was bailiff, in 1542 sheriff of Cupar Angus. In 1491 he sold land in Achnamarkmore to John Stewart. In 1501, he sold land to Eleanore, Countess of Atholl. Baptisms of all his children are in parish register, Cupar Angus. He died at Aughinleyth, Forfashire. He was the father of:

9. James Finley (15 Sep 1530-26 Mar 1597) who married b1576 Elizabeth Warrender, daughter of William and Christina Warrender - Baron's Court Book v 2, p 86. James was born at Cupar Angus. He appears on a list of tenants at Balchristie. In 1574, he received a royal patent to land in Newbern Parish, Balchristie, Fife. He was dean of St. Andrews Presbyterian Church where his children's baptisms are recorded. He died at Balchristie. He was the father of:

10. James Finley (25 Oct 1683-?1643) who married on 14 Jan 1603 Barbara Hunter, daughter of William and Grizelda (Traill) Hunter (See Burke's Landed Gentry). He was born at St. Andrews, Balchristie, Fife. He was a resident of Kirkenbright, Fife. He appears in rental book of Newbern Parish (folio 92) up to 1614. He died at Incharvie, Fife. He was the father of:

11. John Finley (10 Mar 1619-14 Feb 1679) who married 27 Jun 1639 Jane Henning (1621-1674), daughter of Richard and Jane (Smith) Henning. He was born at St. Andrews and died at

Incharvie, Fife. He was a weaver. His children were baptized at St. Andrews. He was the father of:

12. Robert Finley (24 Jan 1652-1698) who married 22 Apr 1672 Ann Saunders (1658-a1719), daughter of John and Mary (Risle) Saunders. He was born at St. Andrews, Incharvie, Fife and died in Glasgow. He was a linen draper in Glasgow. He was a freeman and a contractor for Glasgow-Edinburgh stage line and had shipping interests with his father-in-law. In 1698 letters of administration were given to his widow. He was the father of:

13. Robert Finley (1690-1747) who married on 20 Jun 1721 Catherine Wilkes. He was baptized 22 Apr 1690 at Glasgow, Scotland. He owned "Finley Manor" at Paisley near Glasgow. He was a wool trader and stock breeder. His children were baptized by Rev. Dr. McFarline. His will was proved 20 aug 1747.

Chapter 5

GEORGE FINLEY I

George Finley I (b1735-b1794)
m ? Jane
  1 Robert Finley I (-b1828)
  m 18 Aug 1803 Lucinda Finley d Thomas Finley
  2 John Finley I (-c1829)
  3 George Finley II (b1760-b5 Jan 1836)
  4 James Finley I (a1760-b5 Jul 1841)
  m Nancy Ray (c1775-a1850) d Isaac Ray

We begin our personal family history with
George Finley I whom we first find in official
records of Mecklenburg County, North Carolina
in 1773. He bought land on McKees Creek and
on Caldwell Creek in Mecklenburg County in
1773 and 1775. This land is located east of
Charlotte near the current Cabarrus County
border. McKees and Caldwell Creeks run
parallel courses northward with their
headwaters in current Mecklenburg County and
empty into Reedy Creek in Cabarrus County
which in turn becomes a tributary of Rocky
River. George served as a constable in

Mecklenburg County in 1777. It is likely that George moved to Mecklenburg County from Pennsylvania. His brother John first immigrated to Bucks County, Pennsylvania before 1750. James lived in Frederick County, Maryland in 1758 and probably lived in Pennsylvania before that. It is possible that George immigrated to America about the same time as they. There is a record in the Mormon Library in Salt Lake City that says George was born in 1737 in Dublin, Ireland, but there is no supporting evidence.

About 1788 he moved to Fishing Creek in Greene County, Georgia north of the town of Greensboro, where he bought land from Oliver Porter adjacent to James Akins (Greene Co. DB 1, p. 350) in 1790. Indian Depredation Records in the Georgia Archives show he had three horses stolen by the Indians in 1788. Robert Finley, son and legatee of George Finley Sr. (I), filed a claim for the loss of the horses in 1821. Thus we know Robert was his son and that George died before 1821. Other Indian Depredation claims reveal that James Finley, George Finley II of Walton County and Robert Finley were brothers so all three were sons of George Finley I. John Finley lived on Fishing Creek in Greene County near the other three so he was undoubtedly another son. We have no record of George's death, but in 1794 James Finley and his brother Robert Finley of Greene County, Georgia sold the land which George Finley I had previously bought in North Carolina (Cabarrus Co., NC DB 1, p. 102). It is likely they obtained the land as their share of his estate. There is no mention of George in

29

county records after 1790. Thus George Finley
I must have died between 1790 and 1794.

A widow Jane Finley of Greene County, Georgia
had one draw in the 1805 land lottery. If she
had had children under 21 years of age in
1803, she would have been entitled to two
draws. She won lot 196 of district 24 in
Wilkinson (Pulaski) County in the 1807
lottery. She lived in Greer's district of
Greene County which is also where Robert
Finley I lived. Robert Finley I, son of
George Finley I, paid tax for her on this land
from 1809 to 1811. It is likely she lived
with Robert I and was the widow of George
Finley I. She sold this land in 1811 (Pulaski
Co., DB B, pp. 226-7).

Census records show that George Finley II was
born between 1750 and 1760. James Finley was
born after 1760. We do not have solid
evidence for the birth dates of sons John or
Robert Finley. Since George I had sons born
before and after 1760, we assume he married in
the 1750's, which means he was most likely
born around 1735 or earlier.

There was a George Finley of Salisbury
District, North Carolina, which included
Mecklenburg, who provided food for the
Revolutionary army. This may have been our
ancestor but it also may have been the George
Finley of Guilford County, North Carolina
(brother of Archibald and Michael Finley of
Bucks County, Pennsylvania mentioned in
Chapter 4). There was also a George Finley of
Salisbury District who served in the militia
according to the North Carolina Archives.
This was almost certainly one of our

Mecklenburg County Georges since he gave Capt. Oliver Wylie power of attorney to collect his compensation. Oliver Wylie was a near neighbor of George Finley I in Mecklenburg County. Considering their ages, this was most likely the son, George Finley II, rather than George Finley I.

Mecklenburg County was a center of dissent at the time of the Revolution. Indignant over England's treatment of the colonies, they called for two representatives from each captain's district to meet in Charlotte in convention on 19 May 1775. On 20 May 1775, over a year before the rest of the colonies joined them, Mecklenburg County declared its independence from England. Captain James Jack carried a copy of this declaration to the Continental Convention in Philadelphia. The North Carolina representatives felt the declaration premature and did not introduce it at that time.

The freedom-loving frontiersmen were ready to back up their words with their blood. They volunteered for most of the battles of the Revolution fought in the South. The war came to the frontier area of North Carolina after Gate's defeat at Camden in 1780. Following this defeat the continental army of the south was decimated and there was no organized resistance to Cornwallis. He invaded North Carolina in September and camped at Charlotte, expecting to easily pacify all of the province and bring it under English control.

The local patriotic citizens had other ideas. They effectively resisted English control so that Cornwallis likened his experience in

Mecklenburg County to being in a hornet's nest. After many of his sentries were ambushed and killed, he had them dig pits 5 or 6 feet deep in which to stand in order to reduce their vulnerability. Foraging parties were ambushed and large numbers of troops had to escort them for protection. Couriers were frequently intercepted and killed so that many messages were never received. This active hostility of the civilian population was vastly different from previous wars fought on the Continent. In Europe, civilians pacifically allowed the victorious army to control them, but not so in this war.

Lord Rawdon of the Royal Army sent the following message back to Sir Henry Clinton concerning the period of time when Cornwallis was at Charlotte, "Orders were therefore dispatched to our friends, stating that the hour, [for] which they had so long pressed, was arrived; and exhorting them to stand forth immediately, and prevent the re-union of the scattered enemy. Instant support...was promised. In the fullest confidence that this event would take place, Lord Cornwallis ventured to press your Excellency for co-operation in the Chesapeak, hoping that the assistance of the North Carolinians might eventually furnish a force for yet farther efforts. Not a single man, however, attempted to improve the favourable moment, or obeyed that summons for which they had been so impatient. It was hoped that our approach might get the better of their timidity; yet during a long period, whilst we were waiting at Charlotteburgh for our stores and convalescents, they did not even furnish us with the least information respecting the force collecting against us. In short, Sir, we may have a powerful body of friends in North Carolina - and indeed we have cause to be convinced that many of the inhabitants may wish well to his Majesty's arms; but they have not given evidence enough either of their number or their activity, to justify the stake of this province, for the uncertain advantages that might attend immediate junction with them."

Colonel Tarleton said of Mecklenburg, "Its inhabitants were more hostile to England than any others in America...the foraging parties were everyday harassed by the inhabitants, who did not remain at home to receive payment for the product of their plantations, but generally fired from covert places to annoy the British detachments...Notwithstanding the different checks and losses sustained by the militia of the district, they continued their hostilities with unwearied perseverance; and the British troops were so effectively blockaded in their present position, that very few, out of a great many messengers, could reach Charlotte in the beginning of October to give intelligence of Ferguson's situation."

Cornwallis reported, "it was evident, and had been frequently mentioned to the King's officers, that the counties of Mecklenburg and Rowan were more hostile to England than any others in America. The vigilance and animosity of these surrounding districts checked the exertions of the well-affected, and totally destroyed all communications between the King's troops and loyalists in other parts of the province. No British commander could obtain any information in that position which would facilitate his designs, or guide his future conduct."

This lack of information at English headquarters contributed to the Patriot victory at Kings Mountain. Although Cornwallis with the main body of English troops was only about thirty miles away, he had no knowledge of Ferguson's predicament until after the battle was over. Their victory in this battle encouraged the colonists and many point to this as a turning point of the war. After only 18 days at Charlotte, Cornwallis sought the more congenial climate of Winnsboro, South Carolina.

James Finley of 12 Mile Creek lived within two or three miles of the Jackson family. Andrew Jackson Sr., father of the president, died in the coldest days of February, 1767. The ground was covered with snow and ice had formed on the creeks. Carriages were scarce on the frontier and only one could be found to carry the widow and her children. The corpse was pulled on a sled behind the carriage the twelve miles to burial at the Waxhaw Presbyterian Church in Lancaster Co., South Carolina. James Finley was among the mourners accompanying the procession. He testified they stopped at the creeks to warm themselves with liquor. At the home of George McKemey, a brother in law of Andrew, the group paused for more liquid refreshment. Farther along they probably enjoyed a draught of fine brandy at the home of a prosperous brother in law of Jackson, James Crawford. By now the day was far advanced so they hurried on to the church, arriving at dusk with the sled but no body. The embarrassed band had to retrace their steps to Waxhaw Creek where the body had slid off into the bushes as they had climbed the steep creek bank.

Chapter 6

GEORGE FINLEY II

3 George Finley II (b1760-b5 Jan 1836)
  31 Robert Finley II (b1775-b19 Oct 1811)
  m 26 Nov 1802 Jane Finley in Greene Co., GA
    311 Thomas J. Finley
    m 3 Aug 1846 Nancy Gregory in Greene Co., GA
    Greene Co. WB 5, p. 379
      3111 Thomas L. Finley
    m 19 Aug 1869 Charity A. Crawford in Greene Co, GA
    311.1? Jane Finley
    m 1 Dec 1829 Nowel Crawford in Greene Co., GA
    312 Robert Finley III (c1811-   )
    m Eliza Gregory (c1815-d Gordon & Regie Gregory of Watkinsville), moved to Dallas Co., AR c1861
      3121 Robert Hint Finley (12 May 1837-19 Apr 1908)
      m Nancy E.
        31211 Bob Finley
        31212 Billie Finley

31213 Jackson Finley
31213.1 Lucy Finley
3122 William T. Finley (c1840-   )
m 19 Mar 1865 Mary Evelyn Southerland
   31221 Lewis F. Finley (1866-   )
moved to San Francisco, CA
         31221.1   Hattie   Eugenia
               Finley (12 Feb 1869-
               28 Nov 1963)
     m 11 Dec 1888 Thomas Franklin
       Cheshier
   31222 Crumby Finley (25 Oct 1871-
m Mattie Smith
   31223 James Robert Finley (1878-   )
m 4 Jul 1898 Quinnie Harris
3122.1 Susan Finley (1840-   )
3122.2 Eliza Finley (c1843-   )
m McCoy
3123 Hiram Crumley Finley (c1846-21 Jan 1916)
m Elizabeth Harris
lived Cleveland Co., AR
   31230.1 Belle Finley
   31230.2 Jennie Finley
   31231 Charlie Finley
   31232 Jim Finley
   31233 Ruel Finley
   31233.1 May Finley
3124 John Wesley Finley (1846-   )
   31241 George Finley
   31241.1 Susan Finley
3125 James G. Finley (c1848-   )
m 27 Nov 1863 Mary J. Barnett
   31251 Willie Finley
   31252 John Susil Finley
   31253 Hinley Finley
   31253.1 Dora Finley
   31253.2 Nannie Finley

3126 Joseph D. Finley (c1848-   )
m 1 Jan 1874 Nancy C. Files
  31261 John Finley
  31262 Bert Finley
  31263 Charles Finley
  31263.1 Annie Bet Finley
3127 Iverson Lane Finley (15 Dec 1852-20 Mar 1921)
m Mary J. Mitchell
  31271 Tom Finley
  31271.1 Eliza Finley
  31271.2 Lizzie Finley
  31272 Hiram Finley
3127.1 Mary Laura Finley (c1852-   )
m John W. Barnett
  A Warren Barnett
  B Walter Barnett
  C Emma Barnett
  D Ada Barnett
  E Susie Barnett
3128 Charles A. Finley (1855-   )
m Callie B.
  31281 Clytie Finley
  31281.1 Syble Finley
3129 Franklin Dosia Finley (1858-   )
m Susie

32? Nicholas Finley (c1778-c1817)
m c1803 Elizabeth Middleton d Holland Middleton
moved to Morgan Co., GA, then LA, then Amite Co., MS
  321 John Middleton Finley (17 Dec 1804-21 Sep 1887)
  m 16 Mar 1831 Nancy Guynes (19 Jan 1815-25 Nov 1892)
  lived Scott Co., MS
    3210.1 Martha Caroline Finley (11 Sep 1832-20 Nov 1875)
    m 5 Feb 1851 William Clark (1829-1899)

A John M. Clark (1853-   )
m Laura J. (1860-)
  1 John W. Clark (1875-   )
  2 Mattie C. Clark (1876-   )
  3 Oscar L. Clark (1879-   )
  4 Arra L. Clark (1880-   )
B Mary Clark (1856-   )
m 9 Feb 1878 James Franklin Kilgore
C Nancy C. Clark (1858-   )
m 4 Jun 1878 Alney D. Kilgore
D Elizabeth (Betty) Clark (17 Aug 1860-1946)
m George King (24 Dec 1857-1924)
E William M. Clark (30 Nov 1863-1929)
m 10 Dec 1887 Jennie Madden (1870-1948)
F Jennie Clark (1867-   )
m 8 Sep 1883 M.A. Golden
G Henry Clark (14 Jul 1869- 21 Oct 1940)
m Mattie E.
H Ann Eliza Clark (1871-   )
m 22 Dec 1876 Samuel McNair
3211 Nicholas F.M. Finley (9 Sep 1835-18 Oct 1909)
m 6 Apr 1855 Nancy Mary Jane Spivey
married in Leake Co., MS
m b29 Aug 1859 Mary Johnson
  m a May 1865 Arra J. Coleman d Wm &
      Arra J. Coleman
  32111 Albert Brown Finley (c1859-
m 14 Jan 1883 T.R. Jones in Scott Co., MS
  32112 Nathan E. (Nick) Finley (Oct 1862-
    25 Aug 1938) died Uvalde, TX
m 25 Aug 1887 Sarah Caroline Yates

39

321121 Albert Ross Finley (1888-1950)

m 14 Sep 1915 Willie Lois Cardwell (14 Feb 1885-13 Feb 1990) lived in Uvalde, TX

3211211 Albert Ross Finley Jr. (1916-

m Sue Virginia Johnson (1917-

32112110.1 Sue Virginia Finley

32112110.2 Sarah Eliz Finley

m 1964 Billy Norman Curbow

m 1970 Wm Cecil Weir

m 1976 Karon Gale Campbell

m 1986 Roy Lee Decker

m Donald Wayne Fulton

A Dawn Eliz Curbow (1967-

B Lee Ray Weir (1971-

3211212 Nick Cardwell Finley (1917- m 25 Nov 1949 Ellen Allen

32112121 Nick Cardwell Finley

m 6 Mar 1971 Kay Felts

m 11 Oct 1977 Ann Zimerman

321121211 Blair Finley

321121211.1 Bess Finley

32112122 Deets Eugene Finley

m 1980 Helen "Tina" Jause

321121221 Deets E. Finley

321121.1 Nora O. Finley (1890-1973)

321121.2 Arra M. Finley (1892-1976)

m 14 Mar 1918 Hershel Ray

A Nick Finley Ray (30 Sep1923-1927)

321122 Lonnie Madison Finley (1893-1965)

m Lessey Studer

3211220.1 Callie Mae Finley
(1917-

m 15 Feb 1936 Robt Ingram Allen
  A Robt Wm Allen (19 Oct 1937-
  m 1961 Sally Ruth Surber
    1 Leonard Casey Allen
  B Lewis B. Allen (3 Aug 1939-
  m 1964 Peggy Lynn Shankle
  1 Zane Mitchell Allen
  2 Joel William Allen
    3 Robert Austin Allen
  3211220.2 Betty G. Finley(1921-
  1925)
  321122.1 Betty Eliz Finley (1897-
  1918)
  m 1917 James Elmer Neill in Uvalde
32112.1 Mary A. Finley (1865-   )
m 7 Oct 1878 Joseph M. Sharp s John
T. Sharp
32112.2 Arra Caroline (Callie)
Finley (1867-   )
m 18 Nov 1886 Geo W. Haralson, Scott
Co
A Mary E. Harelson (Apr 1889-)
  B Jessie C. Harelson (Sep 1893-
  C Altey M. Harelson (Nov 1895-
  D Arthur D. Harelson (Mar 1898-
32113 John M. Finley (1869-   )
m 22 Jul 1893 Ellen Davidson, Ellis
Co, TX
321131 Allie Finley (Apr 1894-   )
  321131.1 Effie Finley (Sep 1895-
  321131.2 Ira Finley (Jan 1898-
  321132 Chester Finley (Aug 1899-
32114 James T. (Jessie) Finley
(1871-   )
32115 William H. Finley (Dec 1877-
m Mary   (Nov 1878-   )

321151.1 Addie M. Finley (Jul 1899-   )

32115.1 Nancy Jane (Nannie) Finley (1881-   )

3211.1 Matilda Jane Finley (23 Jul 1836-12Nov 1878

m Elias Jack Madden (1832-   ), Scott Co.

3211.2 Mary Butler Finley (23 May 1838-30 May 1913

m Henry W. Long (1833-1896)

3212 John Guynes Finley (1841-5 Sep 1929)

m Susan Chipley (1842-19 Dec 1912) lived Natchitoches Par., LA

32120.1 Alzadie Arlene Finley (23Dec1861-1931

m 21 Oct 1880 John Henry Fisher

32121 Royal Middleton Finley (29 Apr1866-1940

32122 John Henry Finley (1 Mar 1868-1946)

m 24 Dec 1891 Mattie E. Godwin in Chestnut, LA

321221 Andran Finley (May 1894-

321221.1 Eva M. Finley (Apr 1896-

321221.2 Ula Finley (Mar 1900-

32122.1 Nancy Anna Finley (5 Dec 1871-   )

m David Augustus Thomas

32122.2 Susan Helfredge Finley (1872-

32122.3 Cora Angeline Finley (9 Mar 1873-1952

m 5 Jan 1893 Henry Martin Thomas

32122.4 Martha Harvelia Finley(24Sep1875-1945

m Dec 1894 Gehilah Shelton Regious

32122.5 Rena Carolina Finley (Sep 1876-   )
m James Regious
32122.6 Eunice Delma Finley (6 Mar 1880-   )
m 1900 David Murrel Godwin
32122.7 Edna Victoria Finley (16 Feb 1883-
m 16 Sep 1906 Algon J. Harvey
32122.8 Mary Finley (16 Aug 1884-
m 14 Feb 1904 Charlie Ross Mathews
3212.1 Elizabeth Finley (11 Dec 1842-5 Feb 1882)
m William Anderson Welch (1831-1886)
A William Welch (1859-   )
B Cullen S. Welch (1864-   )
m 21 Sep 1891 Nettie Madden in Scott Co.
C Susie Welch (1871-   )
D Thomas Welch (1874-   )
m 16 Sep 1891 Delia Madden d Joe Madden
E Georgia Welch (1879-   )
m 16 Jan 1899 Will Madden s John E. Madden
3213 Henry W. Finley (3 Mar 1845-6 Oct 1914)
m 12 Oct 1874 Victory Henderson (1874-1890)
Leake Co., MS
32130.1 Nancy A. Finley (30 Jul 1875-1879)
32130.2 Mary E. Finley (1877-   )
m 20 Dec 1899 W.N. Hansen
32131 George William Finley
32132 J. Claude Finley (20 Sep 1885-1911)
32133 James H. Finley

3213.1 Nancy A. Finley (19 Feb 1847-20 Oct 1933)

m Henry J. Johnson s William R. Johnson

A Roxie Johnson

m William Majure

B Mary Johnson

C Dr.W.F. Johnson

m Allie Hartness

D John Johnson

E James Johnson

m Pearl Brantley

F Sallie Johnson

m Majure

m William Gardner

G Carrie Johnson

m W.D. Buntyn

m John Kilgore

3213.2 Ann Eliza Finley (23 Jun 1849-4 Mar 1932)

m Dallas M. Jones s Jessie B. Jones

A Matilda Jones (1868-   )

m 20 May 1901 J. Art Godwin

B Addie Jones (12 Mar 1870-26 Apr 1949)

m 3 Jan 1889 Marshall B. Sharp

C James Jones (1873-   )

m Effie

D Jessie M. Jones (30 Mar 1875-12 Aug 1950)

m 23 Nov 1899 Kate Starling

E William Arthur Jones (1878-   )

m Cleo Sanders

F Percy Jones (13 Feb 1881-15 Apr 1896)

G Annie Jones

m   Underwood

H Dallas Lafayette Jones

m 7 Jun 1918 Zora Jones

3213.3 Sarah Angeline Finley (c1851-
m 18 Jul 1888 William Patrick Edwards
  A Annie Iris Edwards
  m Reginald Miller
  m Charles Snell of Macon, GA
3214 George Brown Finley (1855-1942)
m 28 Jun 1920 Nettie Octarius Mosely
  32140.1 Mary Alice Finley
  m Howard Johnson
  32140.2 Annie Ozell Finley (1913-
  m 18 Jan 1918 Ray Audubon Truitt
  32140.3 Lola Finley (11 Oct 1918-
  m Sturgis Anthony
  32140.4 Nola Finley (11 Oct 1918-3
  May 1958)
  m Herbert Turner
3215 Narcissus Howard Finley (24 Dec 1855-1882)
3215.1 Kitty Ann Finley (1859-   )
m 12 Sep 1875 William G. Dawson (1849-1887)
  A Will H. Dawson (4 Aug 1876-3 Sep 1907)
  B Carl Dawson
  C Jack Dawson
  D Luther Dawson
  E Brownie Dawson
  m Percy Madden s John and Fannie Madden
3216 Jefferson Davis Finley (3 Nov 1861-1878)
321.1 Mary Butler Finley (27 Nov 1806-28 Oct 1862)
m Henry Hall Guynes
321.2 Nancy Finley
m 26 Mar 1829 Thomas C. Scrivenor in Copiah Co.,MS
321.3 Elizabeth Finley

m 14 May 1829 Lewis Lambright in Copiah
Co., MS
322 Nicholas Finley (c1814-   )
m c1845 Alzada Guynes
33? William Finley I (c1783-b8 Jun 1840)
m c1804 Elizabeth Haygood (3 Dec 1788-28 Sep
1879)
lived Clarke, Walton, Monroe Counties in GA
died in Chambers Co., AL
34? Thomas Finley II (c1783-   )
35? Samuel Finley (c1785-   )
m ?   Katherine Grier d Aaron Grier of
Warren Co., GA
35.1? Polly Finley
m 1 Apr 1803 Daniel Stamper in Greene Co.,
GA
35.2? Priscilla Finley
m 22 Sep 1806 Robert Middleton in Clarke
Co., GA
35.3? Nancy Finley
m 12 Sep 1811 Parks Middleton in Morgan Co.,
GA
36 George Findley III (b1796-15 Jun 1853)
m 16 Nov 1826 Lucinda Akins (c1810-1879) in
Morgan Co., GA
lived Freedonia in Chambers Co., AL; died
Coosa Co., AL
   **361 James <u>Lawrence</u> Findley (9 Nov 1827-31
   Dec 1904)**
   m 2 Dec 1847 Jane Angeline Carlisle
   bur Harmony Hill Cem, near Tatum, Rusk
   Co., TX
      3611 Newton Quitman Findley (1848-   )
      3612 Benjamin Griffin Findley (1849-
      3613 Samuel Young Findley (1852-   )
   361.1 Julia Ann Findley (1829-1836)
   **362 Columbus Newton (Cum) Findley (1832-
   10 Mar 1904)**

m 16 Aug 1857 Elizabeth Pate (1838-4 Feb 1930)

bur Hubbard in Hill Co., TX

3620.1 Laura F. Findley (1 Oct 1858-10 Jul 1933)

m Cal Speaker (28 Nov. 1849-7 Nov. 1915)

3621 William Eason Findley (4 Apr 1860-c1923)

m Josephine D. Walton (c1867-c1935)

bur Fairview Cem, Hubbard, TX

36210.1 Annie Elizabeth Findley (1885-1964)

m Ben C. Holman (26 Aug 1886- 3 Jun 1971)

bur Fairview Cem, Hubbard, TX ni

36210.2 Ida Alberta Findley (1886-28 Jan 1967

m 27 Dec 1911 James Albert Wallace (1886-1969) lived Limestone Co., bur Fairview Cem

A Mary Elizabeth Wallace (19 Feb 1913-1994)

m Waller M. Ethridge

bur Marshall, Harrison Co., TX

1 James Thomas Ethridge

B John Findley Wallace (1915-21 Dec 1988)

m 26 Feb 1943 Winifred May Wickenden (1914-1974) bur Fairview, Hubbard, TX

m 6 Mar 1976 Hasseltine F. Whittlesey

1 John Riley Wallace (9 Jun 1944-

m 1969 Mary Ann Gosdin, Oklahoma City

a Karen Wallace (18 Dec 1971-1971)

bur Fairview Cem, Hubbard, TX

        b John David Wallace (18 Jan 1973-

      C James Harold Wallace (1921-5 Jun 1922)

      bur Fairview Cem, Hubbard, TX

      D William Herbert Wallace (24 Apr 1921-

      m Waneta Northern

        1 Mark William Wallace

      36211 James Newton Findley (1889-1951) ni

      m Jesse Evans (1892-1960)

      bur Fairview Cem, Hubbard, TX

   3622 Thomas B. Findley (26 May 1866-

   3623 Joseph H. Findley (28 Aug 1868-1 Sep 1887)

362.1 Mary Walker Findley (1835-1879)

m 4 Nov 1852 Joseph Dupriest in Coosa Co., AL

363 Richard Jones Findley (6 Jun 1838-4 May 1916)

m 27 Sep 1866 Ruth Hickey in Clay Co., AL

lived Columbiana in AL; Harrison Co., TX

   3631 Freedom I. Findley (1867-   )

   3631.1 Nancy Findley (1869-)

   3631.2 Mattie Findley (1871-   )

   3632 J. Walter Findley (1873-   )

   3633 Richard Jenaroso Findley (1875-

   3634 William Joseph Findley (1878-16 Jun 1959)

   m 17 Oct 1902 Viola Phillips in Shelby Co., AL

   died Calera, Shelby Co., AL

   3635 George W. Findley (Feb 1880-   )

   3636 Eugene Findley (Oct 1883-   )

   3636.1 Icie Findley (Feb 1885-   )

   3636.2 Ivie Findley (Oct 1887-   )

363.1 Martha Jane Findley (c1840-6 Jan 1861)

364 Thomas Jefferson Findley MD (1844-16 Dec 1894)
m 13 Jan 1873 Belle Reeder
bur Leaky, TX
365 John Tyler Findley (8 Dec 1846-27 Mar 1917)
m 1867 Charlotte Melinda Pate, Shelby Co ni
m c1875 Martha Graham, Tatum, TX ni
m 2 Jan 1887 Sophie A. Nennstiel (-1891)
bur Oakwood Cem, Waco, TX

  365.1 Effie Lillian Findley (30 Jun 1889-5Dec1971)
  m 31 Dec 1905 Thomas Melton Lewis
  bur Oakwood Cem, Waco, TX

    A Margaret Mae Lewis (11 Nov 1906-26 Oct1972)
    m 9 Jan 1939 John C. King
    bur Oakwood Cem, Waco, TX
    B Thomas Melton Lewis Jr. (9 Nov 1908-
    m 31 Dec 1936 Lillian V. Carr (5 Oct 1912-
    m 7 Jun 1947 Mary Belle Burdette

      1 Brian David Lewis (27 Jan 1938-changed name to John Birch Maylard
      m Pat McAuliff
        a Christopher Maylard (1972-
        b Jeremy Maylard (1976-
        c Jonathan Maylard (1978-
      2 Thomas Melton <u>Tim</u> Lewis (21 Mar 1948-
      3 Mary Margaret Lewis (28 Jul 1950-
    C John Sidney Lewis (22 Sep 1910-
    m 20 Dec 1941 Helen Lucille Kleypas
    D Theresa Josephine Lewis (23 Sep 1913-11 Sep 1914)

    E Nancy Virginia Lewis (2 Aug 1915-
   m 30 Apr 1938 Claude Robert Hunt
    1 Thomas Robert Hunt (17 Jul 1940-
    2 Eugene Lewis Hunt
   F David Findley Lewis (22 Mar 1922-
   29 May 1983)
   m 19 Dec 1959 Ellen Joyce Crocker
   Robinson
    1 Sidney Ellen Lewis (4 Mar 1961-
    2 Nancy Melissa Lewis (18 Aug
    1978-
365.1 Sarah Elizabeth Findley (16 May
1848-23 Oct 1931)
m 28 Feb 1867 A.E. (Bud) Pepper in Coosa
Co., AL
bur Petrolia in Clay Co., TX
365.2 Lucy Ellen Findley (10 May 1851-
1921)
m 15 Jan 1873 Andrew McDonald Richardson
36.1? Rebecca Finley
m 17 Mar 1820 Nathan Hamilton in Clarke Co.,
GA
37 Zachariah Finley (c1803-b11 Nov 1870)
m Martha
m 16 Feb 1856 Lucinda Findley in Shelby Co.,
AL
widow of George Findley III, (# 36)
lived Milltown in Chambers Co., AL; died
Coosa Co., AL
  371? William Finley (c1825-)
  m 1 Jan 1846 Susan Gilliland in Chambers
  Co., AL
   3711 John W. Finley (c1849-)
   3712 Rufus Finley (c1851-)
   ? m 7 Dec 1876 Mary Crawford, Shelby
   Co, AL
   3712.1 Cordelia Finley (c1853-)
   3713 Columbus Finley (c1859-)
  371.1 Symantha Finley (c1827-)

372 George Finley (c1829-   )
m 27 Nov 1855 Margaret Varner in Coosa
Co., AL
373 Leroy Finley (c1833-   )
373.1 Luvinia Finley (c1834-   )
374 Joel Finley (c1838-   )
374.1 Luvinda Finley (c1843-   )
m 3 Aug 1858 John Thomas Wynn in Coosa
Co., AL
37.1 Jane Finley (c1820-   )
37.2 Lockey Finley (c1822-4 Feb 1863)
38?? Jesse M. Finley (c1825- 4 Feb 1863)
lived Chambers Co., AL
38.1?? Martha J. Finley (c1828-   )
m John T. Mathew
lived Chambers Co., AL

George Finley II or perhaps his father served
in the North Carolina militia during the
Revolution. This is indicated by a receipt to
George Finley of Salisbury District for nine
pounds, six shillings specie "for militia
service" on 11 Jun 1783 (Revolutionary Pay
Vouchers, NC Archives).   There were other
George Finleys living in Salisbury District
but we feel sure this voucher refers to our
ancestor because of a notation on it "to Capt.
Oliver Wylie." This seems to indicate George
had Oliver Wylie serve as his agent to pick up
his pay. Oliver Wylie lived on Clear Creek in
the same district in which George Finley lived
in Mecklenburg County, North Carolina.
George's son Robert witnessed a deed involving
Oliver Wylie in Greene County, Georgia, so it
is certain that George knew Oliver. The men
of frontier North Carolina generally did not
serve in the regular army, but raised militia
companies whenever there was a Tory danger or
when the English army was in the area.

Cornwallis invaded western North Carolina in 1780 and camped at Charlotte for about three weeks. It was during this time that George probably served in the militia. Some of the battles in which he may have fought were the Battle of Hanging Rock, of Kings Mountain, of Guilford Courthouse, and skirmishes at Walkup's House and at Ramsuer's Mill. A George Finley of Salisbury District was also paid thirty-nine pounds, four shillings for Revolutionary service, probably for provisions supplied to the patriot army. This could have been one of our George Finley ancestors or perhaps George Finley of Guilford County.

George was living in Greene County, Georgia as early as 1788 when a horse was stolen from him by the Indians (Indian Depredation Claims). He first lived on Fishing Creek in Greene County near his brothers James I, Robert I, and John I and with Thomas Finley I who was probably his cousin. About 1796 he moved across the Oconee River and settled on Greenbrier Creek near Robert Finley II, which is one reason we believe Robert II was his son. He paid tax on 25 acres of land in Greene County and 50 acres of land on Greenbrier Creek in southern Clarke (Oconee) County from 1802 to 1805.

These early days of Greene County were times of Indian troubles. The Indians with some justification believed the land had been unfairly taken from them by the Treaty of Shoulderbone Creek. The only thing separating the Indians from the white settlers was the Apalachee and Oconee Rivers which were easily forded. In 1787 they completely burned every building in the town of Greenesboro, killing thirty-one and injuring twenty people. Charles Finley of another family was killed during this time. The settlers kept their rifles handy as they worked in the fields. At church some would remain outside with their guns, serving as sentries. Sam Dale characterized his life in these early days in Greene County as "inured to every hardship, living on the coarsest food, earning our bread with our rifles cocked and primed, often witnessing the ruin of homesteads and the murder of families, my own life constantly in jeopardy, yet ever hopeful, ever relying on Providence, ever conscious of my duty to my fellow-men, never counting a personal risk for others as a merit, but only as a duty, and, in spite of privation and danger, loving the wilderness to the last."

In 1806 George settled on Sandy Creek in northwestern Morgan County. Nicholas Finley lived within a mile of George in Morgan County from 1808 through 1811. In 1819 George moved westward to the area between Little and Big Flat Creeks in the northwestern part of the new county of Walton. Here he lived near William Finley, being separated by seventeen houses in the 1820 census. At the same time, he lived only three houses from Rebecca Hamilton. Later he is found in Newton County, living near the midpoint of the Newton-Walton County line. He died in Newton County, probably in December of 1835.

George Finley II seemed to rent rather than buy land. He paid tax on land in some locations but no deeds exist in which he bought or sold any of the land. He won 202 ½ acres of land in Houston County in the 1821 land lottery. It is intriguing to speculate why George had so little wealth. Land was cheap and most citizens of the day obtained 200 acres or more in a lifetime. This apparent lack of possessions may mean George was handicapped, either physically or perhaps from alcohol. His relative poverty may also explain why his son William seemed to have financial problems.

Unfortunately no records can by found of a will of George Finley II or of the settlement of his estate. The only record we have is the appointment of Zachariah Finley as administrator of his estate on 5 Jan 1836. Therefore the names of his children must be drawn from inferences. The evidence for some is stronger than for others. Those most strongly associated with George Finley are Robert II, George III, and Zachariah Finley.

Robert Finley II was undoubtedly the oldest son of George Finley II. There were two Robert Finleys in Greene County who registered for the 1805 land lottery. One was designated as Robert Sr. and the other as the son of George Finley. Robert Finley I who lived on Fishing Creek in Greene County was the son of George Finley I but this George had almost surely died before 1794 as noted earlier. It seems unlikely Robert Finley I would be still designated as the son of George Finley ten years later. Also he was the older of the two, so he would have received the designation of senior. The terms senior and junior as used at the time do not necessarily indicate a father and son relationship. The terms simply were used to differentiate two men living in the same community with the same name. They might be father-son, uncle-nephew, or might be completely unrelated. Therefore the Robert Finley on Greenbrier Creek must the one who was "the son of George Finley," meaning George Finley II. George Finley II and Robert Finley II also lived near each other on Joe's Branch of Greenbrier Creek in northwestern Greene County from 1796 to 1805, suggesting they were closely related. Robert Finley first appears on the tax lists in 1796, meaning he was born as early as 1775. This dating is important because it proves George II had children older than the Clarke County Finleys so it is at least possible he could be their father.

George Finley III is the next one we can pretty definitely identify as the son of George Finley II. He first appears in the same tax district as George II in Parkers District of Morgan County in 1817, the two being designated as Sr. and Jr. The only other Finley in the district was John, brother of George II, who had only one draw in the 1805 land lottery. This means he had no children in 1803 when he registered so he could not have adult children in 1817 (He could not be the father of George III). In 1818 George Finley Sr. paid tax for George Finley Jr. so there is no doubt they were father and son. Censuses are confusing as to the date of birth of George III. The 1830 census of Morgan County, Georgia and the 1840 census of Chambers County, Alabama suggest he was born between 1790 and 1800. The 1850 census of Coosa County, Alabama suggests he was born about 1808 but the figures are difficult to read. Virginia Hunt, who is a descendant of George III, has family information to suggest he was indeed born in 1808. He certainly is the George Finley Jr. of the 1817 and 1818 tax rolls of Morgan County. George Sr. (our George II) moved on to Walton County in 1819 but Jr. (our George III) now listed simply as George Finley remains in the same tax district for several more years, some years with Zachariah Finley in the same district. The fact that he paid taxes as early as 1817 means he had to have been born by 1796. In 1826 he married Lucinda Akins in Morgan County.

Zachariah Finley lived next door to George Finley II in Newton County in the 1830 census. He was appointed the administrator of the estate of George II in January 1836, suggesting he was the oldest son still living in the same community at the time of George's death. In addition Zachariah married Lucinda, the widow of George Finley III in 1856. This certainly is consistent with his being a brother of George III and a son of George II. Census information suggests Zachariah Finley was born about 1803.

Many considerations make us think the Clarke County Finleys - William, Nicholas, Samuel, and Thomas II - were also children of George Finley II (See Chapter 13 for more information on the Clarke County Finleys). The following numbered, indented paragraphs contain the information which makes us feel the Clarke County Finleys are also children of George Finley II.

> 1. The dates are consistent. George Finley II had a son born by 1775 and the next known son was born about 1796. No other Finleys in the area seem to be his children with the

exception of Polly Finley who married Daniel Stamper in Greene County in 1803. Daniel Stamper lived in the same tax district as George Finley II so she may well be his daughter. Still there is a tremendous gap between his first and second known children and the Clarke County Finleys fill this gap very well and in fact fit snugly. This cannot be said for any other Finley who lived nearby.

2. The physical factors are consistent. George Finley II lived near the southern border of Clarke (Oconee) County and paid tax on land on Greenbrier Creek in southern Clarke (Oconee) County from 1802 to 1805. The only other Finley owning land in Clarke County was Thomas I who can be excluded as the father of the Clarke County Finleys. This places George Finley II physically close to the Clarke County Finleys at the time they first appear in the records and at the time they appear to be leaving home. Nicholas Finley lived within a mile of George II in Morgan County from 1808 to 1811 and William Finley lived seventeen houses away from George II in Walton County in 1820. Nathan and Rebecca Hamilton lived only three houses from George Finley II in the 1820 census. In addition, Nathan Hamilton lived next to Aaron Hopkins and Aaron Hopkins paid his tax for him in 1819. Aaron Hopkins earlier

lived on Greenbrier Creek in southern Clarke (Oconee) County next to George Finley II (Clarke Co. DB D, P. 65). We can closely connect Nathan Hamilton with George Finley II. Thus we find one or another of the Clarke County Finleys in close proximity to George Finley II over a period of almost twenty years.

3. William Finley and the Fishing Creek Finleys of Greene County, one of which was George Finley II, were all closely connected with the Rays. William witnessed a deed of sale for land in Morgan County by Joseph Ray in 1816 (Morgan Co. DB F, p. 161). Joseph Ray was the son of Joseph Ray (Sr.) who had lived on Freemans Creek in Clarke (Oconee) County, and who is likely one of the Joseph Rays who lived on Fishing Creek in Greene County in the 1790's near George and the other Fishing Creek Finleys. Also Mahala, oldest daughter of William Finley married Elisha Ray after the families had moved to Monroe County, Georgia. Elisha had married his first wife in Oglethorpe County where he lived in the early 1820's. Elisha Ray at one time owned land on Fishing Creek in Greene County (Greene Co. DB JJ, p. 254). He was taxed in the Fishing Creek district of Greene County in 1825 - the same district in which lived James and Margaret Finley (widow of Thomas I) and where George Finley II had previously lived. The

Fishing Creek Finleys were very close to the Rays. James Finley was the son in law of Isaac Ray. John Finley, the brother of George II, married Mary Ray in Greene County in 1804.

4. Many of the business associates of William Finley I lived in the southern part of what is now Oconee County which suggests he had an orientation toward Greenbrier Creek where George Finley II had his land. Harmon Runnels who loaned William money in 1803 (Clarke Co. Superior Court Records) lived on Rose Creek which flows parallel to and two or three miles east of Greenbrier Creek. Harmon also had business interests in northern Greene County (Greene Co. Court Records). William served as the assignee of Stephen Nobles to collect a debt (Clarke Co. Superior Court Records). Stephen Nobles lived on Greenbrier Creek in Clarke (Oconee) County. William Finley cosigned a note for John Brewer in 1803 (Clarke Co. DB A, pp. 117-8). The note also reveals they had an arrangement whereby John Brewer was to collect one-third of the next crop from William Finley's farm. John Brewer was apparently the son of Hundley Brewer who lived on Calls Creek, the only Brewer living in the same tax district of Clarke County as William Finley. Hundley had first lived on Greenbrier Creek in Clarke County

and in 1793 he appeared on a jury roll in Greene County.

Estate papers of Robert McAlpin, who lived on Wolfe Creek in the southwestern portion of present Oconee County (near Greenbrier Creek), in <u>Clarke County Administration of Estates Returns 1799-1819</u>, pp. 178-9 in November 1804 show that George Finley II owed money to McAlpin as well as participated in the estate sale. Stephen Nobles and Howell W. Runnels were also mentioned in the estate papers. There is evidence Howell W. Runnels was related to Harmon Runnels and was probably his son. Thus we have evidence that George Finley II and William Finley I had common acquaintances.

5. The Clarke County Finleys and George Finley II all had connections to the area just west of Washington in Wilkes County. Nicholas Finley was taxed in this area in 1802 and probably lived there when he registered for the land lottery in 1803. We have noted William Finley's connection to Hundley Brewer. Hundley Brewer's brother Caleb lived in the same district. Hundley himself sued Bedford Brown who lived there. Powell Stamper lived in the same region and served as administrator of the estate of Caleb Brewer. Daniel Stamper was probably a son of Powell and he also

lived in the same area in the 1790's. About 1798 he moved to Greene County where he lived in the same tax district as George Finley II. In 1803 he married Polly Finley who was probably the daughter of George Finley II. We can imagine a situation in which Nicholas as the son of George Finley II became friends with Daniel Stamper and through him learned of a job opportunity in the Washington area of Wilkes County.

6. When Thomas Finley I sold land on Greenbrier Creek in 1798 (Jackson Co. DB A-B 1796-1800, p. 208) the county clerk mistakenly wrote in the place for the signature "William Finley." This suggests there was a William Finley closely related to Thomas Finley. Thomas had a son named William C.H. Finley, but he was a child of eight or nine at the time. It is more likely the clerk was thinking of a son of George Finley II. Thomas at the time was selling two tracts of land to Aaron and Samuel Hopkins. Immediately after the land was transferred in 1800, George Finley II paid tax on land on Greenbrier Creek in Clarke County (Clarke County was formed out of Jackson County after the sale) adjacent to Hopkins. It seems likely this land is part of the land Thomas sold in 1798 (actually for some unknown reason the sale did not become final until 1800. There is

another deed for the same sale recorded in Clarke County deeds). We can imagine that George Finley II was already renting this land from his cousin, Thomas, on a more informal basis before 1798. George's name never appears in Clarke (Oconee) County tax records, so he lived all the time in Greene County. It is reasonable to assume that he had his teenage sons farming the land in Clarke (Oconee) County in 1798. When they became old enough to move out on their own, they settled around Watkinsville, where we find the Clarke County Finleys.

7. William Finley I and Reuben Boothe together borrowed money in 1803, suggesting they were close friends at the time William was first moving out on his own. This suggests that Reuben was from a family that were friends with William's family. Clarke County Superior Court records show that Reuben was confined in the Oglethorpe County jail in 1805, suggesting he lived in that county before moving to Clarke County. Reuben witnessed a deed in which John Boothe bought land on the headwaters of Long Creek in Oglethorpe County (Oglethorpe Co. DB G, p. 4), located near land owned by Thomas Finley I. The land Boothe bought was adjacent to the Gillum's, who were in laws of Thomas Finley I.

We know Thomas Finley I was not the father of the Clarke County Finleys, but this connects them with a near relative of George Finley II.

8. There are several factors which could explain how a son of George Finley II could have moved to Barbers Creek and could have been acquainted with the Haygoods. Jesse Jenkins and George Calhoun lived on Greenbrier Creek in Greene County near George II and also owned land on Barbers Creek in Clarke (Oconee) County, suggesting a movement of settlers in that direction.

Lambreth Hopkins and Daniel Bankston were neighbors in Stanley County, North Carolina at the time of the Revolution. It is possible they were acquainted with the Mecklenburg County Finleys at that time. Both moved to southwestern Wilkes County, Georgia in the 1780's where they became neighbors of Alexander Autrey. In the 1790's Daniel Bankston lived as a next door neighbor to Benjamin Haygood in Hancock County. Lambreth Hopkins and Alexander Autrey both moved to the Fishing Creek area of Greene County where they certainly knew George Finley II. All three of these men moved to Clarke (Oconee) County and all three were connected with the Mars Hill Baptist Church. Alexander Autrey and Daniel Bankston lived in the southern part of current Oconee County and served on the founding council of the church. Alexander Autrey also witnessed the will of Daniel Bankston in Morgan County so we know they were friends. Lambreth Hopkins' widow Prucilla was one of the charter members of the Mars Hill church. These relationships show that George Finley II and Benjamin Haygood had mutual friends who could have served to introduce their children.

John Stroud Jr., whose brother Mark Stroud was father of three children who married children of Benjamin Haygood, lived after 1793 in the Richland Creek area of southwestern Greene County. About 1798 he moved to the Greenbrier Creek area of Greene County where he was a neighbor of George Finley II. About 1802 he moved to the Robinsons Creek area of Clarke (Oconee) County where he was a neighbor of Samuel and Nicholas Finley. In other words John Stroud was acquainted with George Finley II as well as Benjamen Haygood.

Evidence from censuses suggests George Finley married at least three times. One might suspect that Robert II was the oldest and George III the youngest children of the first wife. There is a fairly large gap between the births of George III and Zachariah and no other possible children of George Finley II seem to fit into this time frame. Zachariah Finley probably was the oldest son of the second marriage and perhaps several children unknown to us were also of this second wife. An unnamed female who was married to Thomas Bird may be one of the children of the second marriage. Thomas Bird lived adjacent to George II and Zachariah Finley in 1830 and he served as bondsman when Zachariah was appointed administrator of the estate of George Finley II. George had children under five years of age in his house in 1830 and the oldest female was under thirty. He may have married a young woman in his old age and sired a third set of children. Of course these could be grandchildren living in his house. If he had young children in 1830, Martha the wife of John T. Mathew may have been one of the youngest children. Nancy Finley who lived in the house with John T. and Martha in Chambers County, Alabama in 1850 may be George's widow.

Robert Finley II lived on Greenbrier Creek in Greene County until his death in 1811. Nicholas Finley lived in Wilkes County in 1802 and 1803. He lived on Barbers Creek or possibly Robinsons Creek in Clarke County from 1804 to 1808. He lived in Morgan County until 1811 when he moved through Louisiana to southwestern Mississippi. In 1813 he was taxed in Marion County, Mississippi, then moved on to Amite County. Tradition says he died in a hunting accident in 1817. Nicholas married Elizabeth Middleton, daughter of Holland Middleton (died in 1795) who lived on Shoulderbone Creek in Hancock County. After Nicholas' death she married John Whittington and they moved to Copiah County, Mississippi.

Thomas Finley II disappears from the tax lists after 1813. Samuel Finley lived in the Robinsons Creek area near Nicholas for several years. He lived in northern Morgan County in 1808 and 1809 and in the Trail Creek area of Clarke County near Thomas in 1810 and 1811. We have one mention of him in Morgan County again in 1813 and he then disappears. Family records of the family of Aaron Grier of Warren County, Georgia state his daughter Katherine married a Samuel Finley. Aaron's will names a daughter Katherine Finley. The only available Samuel Finley living in the area is our Clarke County Samuel so he may be the son in law of Aaron Grier.

George Findley III lived in Morgan County, Georgia into the 1830's. About 1835 he moved to the Freedonia Community in Chambers County, Alabama. He may have lived for a short time in Rock Mills in Randolph County where family tradition says son John Tyler Findley was born. By 1850 he had moved to Coosa County, Alabama where he owned a mill. He died in a mill accident in 1853.

Zachariah Findley lived in Newton County, Georgia in 1840, the Milltown community of Chambers County, Alabama in 1850 and in Coosa County, Alabama afterwards. He married Lucinda, the widow of George III, in 1856 in Shelby County, Alabama.

Chapter 7

WILLIAM FINLEY I

33 William Finley I (c1782-b8 Jun 1840)
m c1804 Elizabeth Haygood (3 Dec 1788-28 Sep 1879)
   330.1 Mahala Finley (c1805-   )
   m 30 Dec 1827 Elisha Ray (b1800-b5 Oct 1840)
     A Elizabeth Ray (c1833-   )
     B Frances Ray (c1835-   )
     C William Ray (c1838-   )
   331 Augustus H. Finley (7 May 1806-25 Jan 1888)
   m c1830 Martha A. Powell d William Powell
   m 20 Aug 1848 Mary Ann Hines Holt (15 May 1816-2 Mar 1894)
   d Thomas Hines of Troup and Greene Cos., GA
   332 Alfred B. Finley (c1810-   )
   332.1 Mary Finley (11 Aug 1811-18 May 1853)
   m b1830 William Foster (22 Oct 1801-18 Nov 1879)
     A James Foster (c1839-   )
     B Frances <u>Marion</u> Foster (c1841-   )
     C Alfred Foster (c1843-   )
     D Mary Foster (c1846-   )

    E Nancy (Margaret) Foster (c1848-   )
    F Sara Foster (c1850-   )
    G Augustus Foster (c1852-   )
333 William A.J. Finley (c1815-? b1860)
?   same as James Finley
?   m 17 Dec 1842 Mary A.M. (Mariah) Akins
    3330.1 Martha Finley (c1840-   )
    3331 Thomas Finley (c1841-   )
    3332 James Finley (c1843-   )
    332.1 Elizabeth Finley (c1847-   )
    3333 Zachariah Finley (c1852-   )
    3333.1 Paralee Finley (c1854-   )
    3334 George Finley (c1857-   )
333.1 Nancy M. Finley (8 Jan 1817-16 Mar 1896)
m Richmond Pearson (5 Nov 1813-16 Jul 1900)
    A Sara A. (? E.) Pearson (c1837-   )
    m 8 Feb 1855 Nathan E. Bozeman
    B Benjamen Pearson (c1838-   )
    C John W. Pearson (c1840-   )
    D William H. Pearson (c1842-   )
    E Christopher Columbus Pearson (c1844-
    F Richmond M. Pearson (c1847-   )
    G Mary A. Pearson (c1849-   )
    H Samantha C. Pearson (13 Sep 1850-10 Apr 1905)
    m Joel H. Weaver (22 Sep 1851-6 Sep 1919)
    bur Freedonia Church, Chambers Co., AL
        1 Rebecca Weaver
        2 James Weaver
        3 George Weaver
    I Rebecca Pearson (c1852-   )
    J James Monroe Pearson (c1854-1912)
    m Mary Jane (Janie) Tucker (1855-   )
        1 Margaret Pearson
        m Ben Frazer
        2 Ada Pearson
        m Lee Headley
        m Will B. Nichols

 3 Anna Pearson
 m Clifton C. Fuller
 4 Sara Katherine Pearson (1891-1948)
 m Lee Penn Montgomery (-1917)
 m Otis DeWitt Alsobrook Sr. (1882-1947)
   a Mary Jane Montgomery (1915-
   m Wood Dozier
   b Otis DeWitt Alsobrook Jr. (1920-
   c Sue Pearson Alsobrook (1923-
   d John Nathaniel Alsobrook (1927-1976)
   e James Pearson Alsobrook (1930-
 5 John Quincey Pearson
  K George F. Pearson (c1856-   )
 333.2 Elizabeth Finley (c1827-   )
 m 19 Sep 1844 Frederick Swint
 s Frederic and Rebecca Harris Swint, he was
 PB preacher
   A John G. Swint (c1846-   )
   B William F. Swint (c1849-   )
   C Sara Swint (c1851-   )
   D Jackson F. Swint (c1853-   )

William Finley first appears in the tax list of Clarke (Oconee) County, Georgia in 1803. This would suggest he was born by 1782. He did not have a draw in the 1805 land lottery which probably means he was not born before 1782. The rules for this lottery stipulated any resident over 21 years of age who had lived in Georgia for one year was entitled to at least one draw.

He bought 200 acres of land on Barbers Creek northwest of and near the town of Watkinsville in 1803. Clarke County DB A 1802-1804, p. 117-8 suggests he was operating on a shoestring. It seems John Brewer had paid an unspecified amount of the sale price of the land which entitled him to one - third of the next year's crop. William also cosigned a note so John Brewer could buy a fine horse. John promised him a black horse blind of one eye, one rifle gun, and relinquished his 1/3 interest in the next crop if he failed to repay the note. William seems to have had plenty of ambition. He purchased two slaves, wintered stock for the county, and tried to collect a note for Stephen Nobles. However he was overextended and several times in these early Clarke County days others sued him to collect debts. In 1807 there was an extremely severe drought which set William back. He was listed as a defaulter on his taxes in 1808 and he never again paid tax on the 200 acres or on slaves. He appears to have lost both. He did not own land again until he won 500 acres in Early County in the 1820 land lottery.

William also had a carpentry shop. Samuel Finley worked several months for him and had to sue him to collect his wages. Superior Court records reveal Nicholas Finley owed William money and William turned this note over to Samuel as partial payment of the suit. These records strongly hint all three were related and probably were brothers. There are also a couple of suits in which William had to go to court to collect money owed him for carpentry work done for others. We should remember that cash was extremely short at this period of history which at least partially explains why William and many others had difficulty paying their debts. Ferrol Sams description of a farmer-carpenter in his book, The Passing Stories probably fits William Finley, "A man who could patch a broken door, put a new spoke in a wagon wheel, replace a rotted board on the barn, or make brand-new steps for the front porch was a plain ordinary farmer. A farmer with extra skills that he more than likely had learned from his father, one who knew how to lay out a foundation, erect a building and put a roof on and who also had the equipment as well as the knowledge, was respected as a carpenter."

William and Nicholas Finley were both members of the Mars Hill Baptist Church which further suggests they were brothers. It was undoubtedly in church that William met Betsy Haygood, daughter of deacon Benjamin Haygood. Elizabeth's name was still Haygood when she joined the church on 13 Jun 1803. Their first child was born in 1805 so it is likely they married late in 1803 or early in 1804. Marriage records in Clarke County are not complete until after 1805 so there is no official record of the marriage. William was excluded from the church membership on 16 Nov 1805 but Elizabeth continued a member in good standing.

Nicholas Finley was taxed in Clarke County in 1804 but is missing in 1805. He reappears in 1806 in the same tax district in which William had previously lived. William was not listed in 1806 but came back in 1807. Nicholas was granted a letter of dismission from the church on 19 Jan 1805 and had rejoined before Nov 1806. Elizabeth Finley was dismissed on 15 Feb 1806 and rejoined on 18 Apr 1807. These combinations of facts suggest Nicholas moved in 1805 into the developing territory of what is now Morgan County which had recently been taken from the Indians and where work clearing land or building buildings was easily obtained. He returned in 1806 to farm William's land in Clarke County and William then probably spent the year of 1806 working in Morgan County.

William Finley then lived on Barbers Creek near his in-laws until 1818 or 1819 when he moved to the newly developed county of Walton where he lived 17 houses from George Finley II in the 1820 census. George lived between Little and Big Flat Creeks. There was an Elizabeth Finley who was a founding member in 1820 of the Sardis Baptist Church which was located one or two miles east of Big Flat Creek. It seems both families lived northwest of the town of Monroe within a few miles of each other.

William lived for a few years in the 1820's in DeKalb County, Georgia. He apparently was still overextended financially for his father-in-law, Benjamin Haygood, had to sue him to collect on a debt.

By 1828 William had moved to the Strouds Crossroads Community in the southwest part of Monroe County where he again lived near Elizabeth's parents and siblings. In 1834 he paid tax on 101 ½ acres of pine land in district 11, lot 40. In 1838 he and Augustus Finley were listed as residents of Wickersville, about six miles east of Lafayette in Chambers County, Alabama. He died in Chambers County before 8 Jun 1840. The division of his estate is recorded in Chambers County Settlements Book I, pp. 148-9. Following the death of William, Elizabeth moved to the Freedonia Community where she bought 320 acres of land east of Freedonia very near the Georgia line. Half the land was bought from William Bledsoe who died without giving her a clear title to the land. She had to sue his administrator, Britton Stamps, and did not receive clear title until 1849. A good portion of this land is now covered by the backwater of the West Point dam. In 1842 Elizabeth was taxed for 7 slaves and for one non-metal clock.

It seems Elizabeth was a woman of ambition and determination. It is interesting in the settlement of her father's estate, all her sisters signed with a mark but Elizabeth was able to sign her name. This was in a time when many men and most women were unable to read and write. When Elizabeth had to break up housekeeping she moved in with daughter Nancy Pearson and on 11 Oct 1873 she joined her church, the Macedonia Primitive Baptist Church, where she is buried. She had previously been a member of the Sharon Primitive Baptist Church which was located near Freedonia on the road to Lafayette.

Elizabeth was the daughter of Benjamin Haygood, a respected member of his communities in Clarke and Monroe Counties. He owned hundreds of acres of land in the Barbers Creek area. He frequently served as foreman of juries. He was an early member of the Mars Hill Baptist Church where he was elected a deacon on 31 Jan 1801. In Monroe County he was a deacon of the Sharon Baptist Church.

Benjamin Haygood (20 Jun 1758 - 4 Jan 1841) was born in Orange County, NC and died in Monroe County, GA. He lived in Chatham County, NC in 1775 when he enlisted in the North

Carolina militia for the Revolutionary War. He served in Capt. George Hendon's and Capt. Wilcox's companies of General Folsom's Regiment (National Archives # R4789). He married Mary Stewart 24 Dec 1777. Mary was the daughter of James Stewart, also a Revolutionary soldier. He was born in Virginia in 1737 and died in Chatham County, NC in 1794. His wife was named Elizabeth and their other children were Elizabeth, John, and Jeptha. James Stewart's parents were said to be James and Ann Stewart. Idalyn Stinson found information on James Stewart in <u>Chatham County, 1771-1971</u>, by W. Hadley, D. Goerch Horton, and N.C. Stroud and in <u>History of North Carolina Baptists</u>, vol. 1, 1663-1805, by G.W. Paschal. It seems he was first a member of Deep River Baptist Church. This church disbanded and he and others helped form the Haw River Baptist Church, later known as Old Fork and now as Rock Springs Church. Benjamin Haygood lived in Hancock County, GA before he moved to Clarke County. Both Benjamin and Mary Haygood are buried in the Mars Hill Church cemetery. Their children were:

1. John Haygood (18 Oct 1778-27 Oct 1819)
   m 28 Jan 1804 Mary (Polly) Moss
   Baptist preacher who had many preacher sons.
2. Nancy Haygood (2 Jan 1781-20 Nov 1866)
   m 1800 John Thompson, a preacher
3. James Haygood (25 May 1783-30 Jun 1864)
   m 22 Mar 1807 Sara (Sally) Stroud, ni

4. William Haygood (28 Sep 1785-30 Jul 1849)
   m 24 Mar 1808 Mary (Polly) Stroud (c1791-1873)
   parents of Greene Haygood, lawyer of Watkinsville,
   Georgia. He was father of Atticus G. Haygood,
   prominent Methodist bishop and president of Oxford
   College in Oxford, Georgia. Greene's daughter,
   Laura Askew Haygood, was a Methodist missionary to
   China.
5. Elizabeth Haygood (3 Dec 1788-28 Sep 1879)
   m c1804 William Finley (c1782-b8 Jun 1840)
6. Frances Haygood (16 Jan 1792-29 Nov 1883)
   m 24 Nov 1807 Levi Stroud
7. Sarah Haygood (19 Nov 1795-22 Jun 1868)
   m 13 Aug 1812 Farr Harris Trammell
   buried Freedonia Methodist Church, Chambers Co., AL
8. Benjamin Haygood Jr. (18 Apr 1799-20 Jul 1887)
   m 1823 Frances Middlebrooks Johnston in Jones Co.

The Haygoods were a family of preachers with numerous of their descendants being preachers. They were also a family of remarkable longevity. Benjamin Haygood died at age 83, Mary Stewart Haygood age 91, Nancy Thompson age 95, James Haygood age 81, Elizabeth Finley age 91, Frances Stroud age 91, Benjamin Jr. age 88, and Elizabeth Stewart at age 100.

Idalyn Stinson gives the following as the lineage of the Haygoods: Francis Haygood (Hawkwood, Hogwood, Hawgood, Haughwood) was born about 1620-30 probably in England. He was transported to Virginia in the patent of Richard Tye and Charles Sparrowe on 12 Aug 1650, (Patent Book No. 2, p. 248). On 30 Jul 1670 he was listed in a group of transported persons in the patent of William Pebles in Charles City County on the south side of James River adjoining Mr. Tho. Newhouse and the Burchen Swamp, (Patent Book No. 6, p. 289, also p. 317). Francis settled first in Charles City County where on 5 Aug 1661 he was accused of murder. The charges seem to have been dropped. By 4 Jul 1664 he had moved east to Surry County, Virginia, where he served as a constable. Francis married after 1750 Elizabeth Creed, daughter of Ralph and Grace Creed. He was an heir in 1673 in the estate of Thomas Wall who may have been his wife's grandfather. Francis' will dated 3 Jan 1676, proved 18 May 1677 in Surry County, Virginia names sons Richard, William, and George and a daughter Frances. He also left a silver bodkin to his sister (in law) Mary Creed. He willed that his good friend Lt. Col. Jordan take his son George and his godmother Mary Rome into his care. He signed his will with the mark "H". (The Creeds can be traced back to Gloustershire, England and the Haygoods may have originated there as well).

George Haygood (Hawkwood, Hogwood) was born about 1670 and died in Surry County, Virginia in 1727. His will dated 20 Dec 1727 (probably should be 1726), proved 17 Jan 1727 in Surry County names wife Ann and sons Francis, Richard, George and John. He signed with a mark. Sons George and William were granted land in Brunswick County, Virginia north of the Meherrin River in 1727.

John Haygood, born about 1700-05, died after 1755, obtained 345 acres on the north side of the Meherrin River in Brunswick County, Virginia from William Haygood on 6 Feb 1733. On 2 Mar 1741 he sold 100 acres of this land on the south side of Totero Creek for 5 shillings to younger brother Francis who already lived on the land. In 1755 John Hogwood and son James appear on the tax list of Orange County, North Carolina. A John Haygood, probably his son remained on Totero Creek in Brunswick County, Virginia and left a will dated 13 May 1777, proved 22 Sep 1777. He named wife Mary, sons John, Benjamin, Randal and daughters Elizabeth Collier, Mary, and Rebecca Haygood. The wife of John Haygood Jr. was Mary Lanier, daughter of John Lanier.

James Haygood, born before 1739, died 1768 in Orange County, North Carolina, had a wife named Elizabeth in the proving of his will. His will dated 20 Feb 1768, proved 29 Jul 1768, is recorded in Orange County WB A, p. 83-4. He names sons George, Benjamin, James, and William and daughter Rebecca. William Parten was named executor with his wife and Phillip Gee and George Haygood witnessed the will. The above named Benjamin is the one who moved to Georgia. He sometimes used the name Hogwood in early life but later changed it to Haygood. He signed his Revolutionary War pension application and his will as Hagood but his descendants all spell the name Haygood. In the Revolutionary pension application, Mary Haygood tore out pages from the family Bible and sent them in for proof of her marriage. One of the pages gives us an idea of the type of home remedies they used to treat their ailments. Gravel is an old term for kidney stones and probably often was used for cystitis. Dropsy is an old term for heart failure.

> "medison for the gravil tak hunney bees and dry them in a pot and beet them to powder and pour billing warder to to them one tee cup to one quart of water and drink of it one teecup at time three or fore times a day."

> "medison for the dropsy take the fillings of steel a half of a pound (?) and brimstone beet? ons of these brimstone to gether and wrapt them up together in the fier and burn them well and beet them and put it in one gallon of peech Brandy and drink three spunfuls."

Elisha and Mahala Ray were apparently the first of the family to move to Chambers County, Alabama. Elisha Ray crossed the Chattahoochee River on a ferry at West Point, Georgia as early as 1831. He was the Chambers County auctioneer in 1833.

Alfred B. Finley was appointed Second Lieutenant of Company 539 of the Georgia Militia from 19 Jan 1832 until 29 Mar 1836. He probably remained a bachelor. He lived at

Cusseta in the early 1840's where he may have owned a store. By 1850 he had moved back to the Freedonia area where he lived next to his mother and his widowed sister Mahala Ray. He undoubtedly helped them look after their farms.

William Foster was the son of Jesse Foster and grandson of Kimmie Foster who lived in Wilkes Co., GA before moving to Morgan County, Georgia where he died in 1817. William and Mary Foster are buried in the Freedonia Methodist Church cemetery.

Richmond and Nancy Pearson lived near the Macedonia Primitive Baptist Church in western Chambers County and both are buried there.

There was a James Finley who married Mary A.M. (Mariah) Akins in Chambers County 17 Dec 1842. Censuses and deeds show he lived in Coosa County in 1850. Then he moved to Union County, Arkansas and died before 1860. By that year, Mariah had moved back to Coosa County, Alabama where she lived in the house of Henry Burroughs. The following contains facts which make me think he was the same as William A.J. Finley, the youngest son of William Finley who was named in the estate settlement papers. W.A.J. Finley was born between 1815 and 1820 and James Finley was born in 1815 so the dates are consistent. Lindsey in The Reason for the Tears has recorded patrons for township schools in Chambers County. Each township had a school and local citizens were appointed patrons to oversee the schools. A.B. Finley and W.A.T. Finley served as patrons in the Cusseta township in the early 1840's. Deeds reveal

Alfred B. Finley owned land in Cusseta and he is certainly the same as patron A.B. Finley. Deeds also reveal James Finley and wife Mariah owned land in Cusseta. No W.A.T. Finley is found anywhere else in Chambers County. Anyone who has read handwritten documents quickly realizes a capital T and a capital J look very similar in many people's writing. It seems certain the patron of the Cusseta school was actually W.A.J. Finley and he is likely the same as James Finley who married Mariah Akins. We might also point out that W.A.J. Finley disappears from the records in the early 1840's, the same time James begins to appear. It appears his family called him "William" in his childhood, but when he became a man he preferred his third name "James", and used it thereafter.

Chapter 8

AUGUSTUS H. FINLEY

331 Augustus H. Finley (7 May 1806-25 Jan 1888)
m c1830 Martha A. Powell d William Powell
m 20 Aug 1848 Mary Ann Hines Holt (15 May 1816-2 Mar 1894)
d Thomas Hines, widow of William G. Holt
  3311 William Powell Finley (11 Oct 1831-14 Mar 1897)
  m 11 Sep 1856 Emmaline French Mayo (10 Sep 1835-28 Jun 1905)
  m in Marion Co., GA; bur Freedonia Meth, Chambers Co., AL
    33110.1 Martha (Marsha) Alice Finley (11 Jul1857-) dy
    33111 Robert Lee (Bud) Finley (22 Mar 1859-25 Aug 1927)
    m 13 Jan 1891 Annie <u>Alice</u> Holliday (1858-1929)
    bur Standing Rock Meth. Church, Chambers Co., AL
      331110.1 Vinnie Mae Finley
      m Luther Boman

33112 Oliver Finley (c1859-   )
33113 John Henry Finley (9 Feb 1863-19 Nov 1928)
m Mary J. Sherard, d William D. Sherard
m Sula C. Tomlinson (21 Jan 1878-1961)
bur Bethel Baptist Church, Chambers Co.
 331131 William Sherard (Bill) Finley (1891-1970)
 m 1917 Leola Mae Landrum (1893-1976)
  3311310.1 Katherine Lemerle Finley (1918-
  lived Boaz, AL
  3311311 Wilbur Landrum Finley (9 Aug 1920-
  m 2 Dec 1945 Waynoner Fowler (1973-
  m 7 Nov 1978 Betty Jean Speakman Brown
  lived Decatur, AL
   33113111 Kenneth Wayne Finley (1950-
   m 10 Jan 1977 Barbara Diane Bates
   lives Somerville, AL
    331131110.1 Shannon Leigh Finley 78
    331131111 Nicholas Sean Finley 1979
  3311312 Thomas Edwin Finley (1922-1976)
  m 24 Feb 1946 Cordial Brown
  bur Pine Lawn Natl Cem, Long Island, NY
   33113120.1 Lillian Mary Finley (1946-
   m 1969 Richard James Farrell
    A Richard Thomas Farrell (1970-
    B Donald James Farrell (1972-
    C Danielle Marie Farrell (1975-
   33113120.2 Barbara Ann Finley (1949-

33113120.3 Diana Marie Finley (1852-

m 1972 Barry K. Bower
   A Peter Karl Bower (1973-
   B Scott Thomas Bower (1975-
3311313 Arthur Lee Finley (8 Sep 1925-

m 30 Nov 1946 Alice Lorene Hanner
lived Holly Pond, AL
   33113131 Doyle Wayne Finley (1948-1948)
   33113132 Shelton Lee Finley (10 Jul 1949

   m 2 Jun 1968 Gayle Nell Marchman
      331131320.1 Angela Marie Finley (1969-
      331131321 Terry Lee Finley (1972-
      331131322 Nathan Brian Finley (1976
   33113133 Michael Lynn Finley (1949-

   m 24 Mar 1978 Karon Lynette Meade
3311313.1 Bernice Nell Finley (31 Oct 1928-

m 21 Apr 1966 Eugene Fitzgerald
m 17 Jun 1967 Edward James Plummer
   A Joseph Edward (Joe) Plummer (1965-
   B William James (Billy) Plummer (1966-
3311314 Charles Bernard Finley (3 Apr 1931-

m 11 Feb 1956 Janet Lee McLaughlin
   33113140.1 Geri Kaye Finley (1757-
   33113140.2 Kim Karla Finley (1959-
3311315 John Henry Finley (24 Feb 1934-

m 22 May 1954 Martha Virginia Knight

lives Boaz, AL
>**33113150.1 Vicki Denise Finley** (1955-
>m 30 Sep 1978 William Daniel Welch
>lives Huntsville, AL
>**33113150.2 Sherrie Lynn Finley** (1957-
>m 6 Jun 1976 Michael Foxx
>lives Huntsville, AL
>>**A April Michelle Foxx** (1979-
>**33113150.3 Glenda Annette Finley** (1962-
>**3311316 Samuel Elias Finley** (1934-1934)

331132 James L. Finley (21 Jul 1893-1966)
m Vera Smith
bur near Panama City, FL
>**3311321 Weyman Earl Finley**
>m Ruth Edna Fugate
>lives Jasper, AL
>**3311321.1 Evelyn Finley**
>m Jimmy Vlahas
>lives in CA
>>**A Tom Vlahas**
>>**B Ted Vlahas**
>>**C Jim Vlahas**
>**3311321.2 Hazel Finley**
>m Charlie Garcia
>lives Tucson, AZ
>**3311322 James Willard Finley**

331132.1 Mattie Lou Finley (30 Jul 1897- nm

33114 Rufus Talbot Finley - nm
33115 William Jackson Finley (11 Jun 1866-
m 16 Mar 1893 Arrie Elizabeth Norton
bur Riverdale Baptist, Clayton Co., GA

331151 Joseph **Brewer** Norton Finley (1895-1964) nm

331151.1 Annie Louis Finley (22 Feb 1897-1978) ni

331152 Charlie Haguewood Finley (1898-1922)

bur Riverdale Baptist, Clayton Co., GA

331152.1 Carrie Lee Finley (19 Sep 1900-1 Dec 1900)

bur Riverdale Baptist, Clayton Co., GA

331152.2 Elizabeth (Lizzie) Love Finley (1901-1984)

m 12 Jul 1925 Hugh Elmer Cort (1905-1893)

bur Riverdale Baptist, Clayton Co., GA

  A Mary Elizabeth Cort (6 Sep 1926-ni

    m 20 Aug 1967 Earl Grant (1925-

  B Dorothy Imogene Cort (30 Aug 1931-

    m Wallace Eugene Johnson (-1975)

      1 Anita Elizabeth Johnson (1953-

      m Don Thomason

        a Elizabeth Ann Thomason (1977-

        b Brian Philip Thomason (1982-

      2 Alice Elaine Johnson (1955-

      m Sam Kennison

        a Nathan Wallace Kennison (1976-

        b Lori Jean Kennison (1980-

      3 Janet Leigh Johnson (1960-

331153 Clyde Allen Finley (3 Mar 1903-11 Dec 1969)

m Frances Pate

331154 Clayton Ellie Finley (3 Mar 1903-1987)

m Janie Roundtree

331155 William Mayo (Willie) Finley (1907-1996)

  3311551 Lanny Finley (1953-

  3311551.1 Kay Finley

m Phillips

33116 James Noble Finley (21 Jul 1867-21 Mar 1960) nm

lived Panama City, FL, Ohio, and Ocheltree Co., TX

33117 Emmett Mayo Finley (12 Apr 1868-31 Jul 1937)

m Lola Lee Adams (25 Oct 1877-3 Jan 1961) MD from Southern Medical College, lived Freedonia, AL

    331171 William <u>Polk</u> Finley (29 Sep 1912-

    m 1937 Lorene Vann

    schoolteacher in Rome, GA

        3311710.1 Glenda C. Finley

        m Spencer Willis

          A Derek Willis

          B Vann Willis

        3311711 William Polk Finley Jr. (1940-

        m Justine Dawkins

          33117110.1 Anita Finley

          33117111 Robert William Finley

    331172 James <u>Noble</u> Finley (1916-

    m Leary Bell Doss

    schoolteacher in Rome, GA

        3311720.1 Ann Finley

        3311720.2 Patricia Finley

        m Sam Mays

  33118 Rev. Austin Perry Finley

  m Elizabeth

  33118.1 Polly Finley - dy

3311.1 Mary Ann Finley (c1834-   )

m 17 Jan 1854 John W. Barrow, s Josephus Barrow in Chambers Co., AL

m Grubbs

  A John Barrow - at Susan Merfield P.O., LA in 1888

  B Joseph Barrow - in Magnolia, AR in 1888

3312 Benjamen F. Finley (c1835-   )
m 4 Jan 1869 Lucy A. Wright (31 Oct 1835-6 Dec 1902)
(widow) in Lee Co., AL
3312.1 Frances M. Finley (c1837-   )
3313 Henry H. Finley (21 Sep 1840-8 Jun 1910)
m 18 Oct 1866 P. Genia Ramsey (Aug 1843-8 Jan 1882)
in Troup Co., GA; bur Emory Chapel Meth, Chambers Co., AL
  33130.1 Lee Olea Finley (1869-1953)
  m Wesley McCarley (1861-1928)
    A Calvin McCarley
    B Mary Lorene McCarley
    C John Henry McCarley
    D Sarah Love McCarley
    E Frank Hollingsworth McCarley
  33131 John Edward Finley (25 Jan 1871-8 Jun 1935)
  m 8 Dec 1909 Pearl Reed
  33132 Theodore Walter Finley (10 Mar 1873-13 Mar 1951)
  bur Rock Springs, Chambers Co., AL nm
  33133 Dennis (Dent) Finley (18 Feb 1875-8 May 1944)
  m Etta Underwood
  33134 Frank Finley (4 Nov. 1877-10 Oct 1903)
  33135 Eugene (Dink) Finley (20 Dec 1879-30 Jul 1881)
  bur just west of Dallas, TX at Kileen
  33136 Otis Finley (8 Jan 1882-   )
3314 Josiah C. Finley (c1842-c1879) died in Montgomery, AL
m Margaret F. Hood (c1843-   )   in Montgomery Co., AL
d Baldwin (Baldy) F. and Sarah C. Summerlin Hood

33141 Charles Finley (c1871-   )
ward of T.J. Little in Macon Co., AL in 1888
33141.1 Frances Finley (c1873-   )
lived with aunt Julia C. Gibson in Lee Co. in 1880
ward of uncle S.J. Finley in 1888
33142 Josiah Austin Finley (1879-   )
lived with aunt Julia C. Gibson in Lee Co. in 1880
ward of uncle S.J. Finley in 1888
3315 John Monroe Finley (6 Apr 1844-10 Feb 1920)
lived Lisbon, LA in 1888,? preacher
3316 Augustus Clay Finley (c1847-13 Apr 1913)
m 18 Mar 1873 Mary Ann McClain (14 Oct 1853-2 Dec 1901)
in Chambers Co., AL
corp., Co. C, 6 AL Cavalry, CSA
bur Macedonia Primitive Baptist Church, Chambers Co., AL
   33160.1 Martha (Mattie) Finley (1873-   )
   m Rufus Brooks
      A Rufus Arthur U. Brooks
      m Dora Mae Simmons
         1 Sue Brooks
         m Pat Felton
            a Ronald Dean Felton
            m Jill
               1 Kayla Felton
               2 Taylor Felton
            b Suzanne Felton
            m Gavin Lawson
               1 Chandler Lawson
      B Floyd Brooks (9 Jul 1913-1978)
33160.2 Minnie E. Finley (11 Jan 1876-8 Sep 1942)

m Andrew Jackson Carter (7 Mar 1877-2 Jun 1915)

s C.W. and E.C. Carter

bur Macedonia PB cem, Chambers Co., AL

  A Myrtice Lavorah Carter (21 Oct 1896-14 Jun 1973)

  m 28 Jun 1923 Andrew C. Smith (1889-1960)

  bur Hillcrest Cemetery

    1 Benjamin Lamar (Laing) Smith (4 Nov. 1924-

    m Hazel Gunn

    lives Lanett, AL

    2 Edna Smith nm

    3 Annie Belle Smith

    m James O. Hart

      a Ronald Hart

      b Gerald Hart

    4 James Harrison Smith

    m Virginia Crouch

      a James H. Smith Jr.

      m Nina Niaman Spurrier

        1 Christine Smith

        2 Elizabeth Smith

        3 James Daniel Smith

      b Judith Virginia Smith

      m Timothy W. Ware

        1 Christine Elizabeth Ware

  B Mary Edna Carter (13 Jul 1902-4 Aug 1987)

  C Annie Belle Carter (2 Feb 1910-5 Oct 1977)

    m 16 Nov. 1929 James Olin Hart (1909-1994)

    bur Oakwood Cemetery

      1 James Ronald Hart (29 Nov. 1933-

      lives Lanett, AL

> > > 2 **Gerand Wayne Hart** (30 Jun
> > > 1936-
> > > lives Pigeon Forge, TN
> > > > a **Roger Carter Hart**
> D **James Harrison Carter (23 Feb 1915-11
> Aug 1986)**
> m 17 Nov. 1940 Virginia Kathryn
> Crouch (1917-
> bur Tucker, GA, managed hardware in
> Atlanta
> > 1 **James Harrison Carter II (4 Jul
> > 1945-
> > > m Nina Niaman Spurrier
> > lives Ft. Lauderdale, FL, grad GA
> > Tech
> > > > a **Christine Elizabeth
> > > > Carter**
> > > > m Martins
> > > > b **James Daniel Carter**
> > 2 **Judith Virginia Carter** (13 Aug
> > 1951-
> > > m Timothy Ware
> > lives Cumming, GA
> > > > a **Christine Kathryn Ware
> > > > lives VA**

33161 **Augustus Haygood Finley (19 Sep
1877-Dec 1946)**
m 12 Dec 1900 Elah Lamyrle Roberts (1878-
1913)
m Daisy Holderidge (1878-1916) (2 sons)
m Mary Jane (Mollie) Mann (1888-1960) (4
sons)
bur Mt. Zion Cem, Ashland, Clay Co., AL
> 331611 **Byron Bruce Finley (26 Aug 1901-
> 5 May 1981)**
> m May 1926 Lucille House (8 Sep 1899-
> 1992)
> d Anthony Crumbley and Zora Dixie Berry
> House

Primitive Baptist preacher and Sup. of Ed.
lived Lineville, Clay Co., AL
   3316111 Wayne House Finley, MD (7 Apr 1927-
m 6 Jul 1952 Sara Will Crews, MD (1930-
d J.B. and Jessie Mathews Crews
both pediatricians and geneticists, UAB
      33161111 Randall Wayne Finley, MD (1956-
   33161111.1 Sara Jane Finley (1960-
3316111.1 Dixie Lamyrle Finley (1929-
m Lester Greene Roberts (1926-1998)
      A <u>Janice</u> Roberts (1957-
      B <u>Donald</u> Lester Roberts (1960-
m 3 Mar 1984 Laura Smith in Covington Co., AL
      1 Benjamin Bradley Roberts (1988-
      2 Eric Wesley Roberts (1990-
      3 Samuel Garrett Roberts (1993-
      C Carol Roberts (1961-
      D <u>Steven</u> Finley Roberts (1964-
m Carol Anne Gillilan (1966-
      1 Anna Caroline Roberts (1999-
3316112 Robert Byron Finley (1935-
m Martha Stone
m Myra Younger (1944-
   33161121 Michael Finley (1965-
      m Leisa (1967-
   331611210.1 Carly Finley (1995-
   331611211 Austin Finley (1998-
   33161121.1 Kelly Finley (1968-
      m Kenneth Lever (1963-
         A Kira Michelle Lever (1997-

331611.1 Mary Ann (Manna) Finley (6 Mar 1903-1912)
bur Mt. Zion cem, Clay Co., AL
331612 James <u>Austin</u> Finley (25 Oct 1906-1935)
bur Mt. Zion cem, Clay Co., AL
331613 Wyatt Horace Finley (12 Jul 1910-
m 4 Apr 1936 Katherine Lowe (14 Aug 1914-
d William Commodore and Ella C. Watley Lowe
lives Marietta, GA and Fitzgerald, GA
  3316130.1 Kathryn Wylene Finley (22 Apr 1948-
  m 18 Jul 1970 James Lamar Stone
  lives Fitzgerald, GA
  A James Lamar Stone, Jr. (22 Aug 1978-
    B William Jeremy Stone (14 Feb 1985-
331613.1 Anna Dora Finley (23 Jan 1913-1917)
bur Mt. Zion Cemetery, Clay Co., AL
331614 Byrle Finley (16 Apr 1916-16 Oct 1916)
331615 Earl Finley (16 Apr 1916-1916)
331616 Raymond <u>McClain</u> Finley (17 May 1919-
m Madge Murphree
lives Birmingham, AL
  3316161 Ray Bruce Finley (1958-
331617 Marion Harris Finley (13 Oct 1921-
m Geneva Davidson
lives Ashland, AL
  3316170.1 Patsy Finley (1950-
  m Don Sullivan
    A Stacy Sullivan

3316171 Donny Finley (1952-
m Janet
he is an artist, lives in
Birmingham, AL
   33161710.1 Catie Finley
   33161710.2 Leah Finley
   33161710.3 Sarah Finley
**331618 Augustus Haygood Finley Jr. (11
Mar 1929-**
lives Birmingham, AL
**331619 William (Billy) Jasper Finley (3
Nov. 1930-**
m Shirley Jeanette Collier
   3316190.1 Susan Finley
   m   Srygley
   lives Helena, AL
     A Chris Srygley
   3316191 William David Finley
   lives New Haven, CN
   3316191.1 Michelle Finley
   m   Rider
   lives Helena, AL
     A Kayla Rider
   3316191.2 Rebecca Finley
   m   Howard
   lives Oneonta, AL
     A Chip Howard
     B Shannon Howard
   **3316192 Thomas Jefferson (Jeff)
Finley**
   lives Calera, AL
**33162 James (Jim) Horace Finley (20 Sep
1879-5 Jan 1928)**
m 14 Dec 1904 Lillie Odessa Smart Sharpe
(1882-58)
   **331620.1 Emma <u>Irene</u> Finley (29 May
1906-1972)**
   m 25 Dec 1926 Homer Lee Owens (1900-
   A Weyman Byron Owens (19 May 1927-

B James Olin Owens (23 Apr 1929-
C Robert Earl Owens (6 Mar 1931-
D Royce Roland Owens (2 Jul 1932-
1932)
E Kerry Eugene Owens (27 Jan 1934-
F Horace Monroe Owens (4 May 1935-
G Alan O'Neal Owens (27 Apr 1937-
H William Hoyt Owens (19 May 1939-
I Doyle Donnelle Owens (6 May 1941-
J Darius Donald Owens (2 Feb 1943-
K Walter Lee Owens (23 Jul 1944-
L Doris Irene Owens (Apr 1947-
M Farris Lanelle Owens (Mar 1949-
N Marvin Dana Owens (4 Aug 1951-
331621 Leonard Sharpe (Slim) Finley (1907-1983)
m Mary Jane Britt (8 Jun 1909-
bur Oakwood cem, Lanett, AL
   3316210.1 Ruby Blanche Finley (26 Aug 1927-
   3316210.2 Barbara Ruth Finley (14 Jun 1929-
   3316211 Charles Hugh Finley (1 Jan 1934-
   3316212 Richard Royce Finley (29 Mar 1937-
   3316212.1 Carol Yvonne Finley (7 Feb 1941-
   3316212.2 Linda Sue Finley (31 Aug 1944-
331622 James <u>Clyde</u> Finley (21 Jun 1912-2 Jul 1996)
   m Apr 1931 Miriam Holle (18 Jan 1909-
d Charles & Bernice Freeman Holle
m Estell J.
he operated florist shop in La Grange, GA
bur Holly Hill Meml Park, Fairburn, GA

3316221 James Clyde Finley Jr. (17 Jan 1935-

      m 3 Jul 1960 Louise Young

      lived Atlanta, GA

  33162210.1 Holle D. Finley (15 Apr 1964-

3316222 William Charles Finley (13 Jan 1937-

    m 4 Aug 1961 Ellen Jennette Jerkins (16 Nov. 1937- d Fordie and Blanche Fincher Jerkins

lived Atlanta and Savannah, GA

  33162220.1 Tina Jennette Finley (1963-

  m 1984 Donald Justin Myers, Jr

    A Brittany Lorraine Myers (1987-

    B Alyssa Jennette Myers (1995-

33162220.2 Martha Leigh Finley (1964-

  m 1991 Hansel Brodrecht Hart (1963-

lives Columbia, SC

    A Christine Elizabeth Hart (1996-

33162221 William Charles Finley Jr (1969

  m 30 Nov. 1996 Kristin Noriko Nakano

    331622211 Austin Nakano Finley 1999

33162222 James Patrick Finley (1972-

  m 1998 Dawn Eileen Faehnrich (1968-

3316222.1 Jane Finley

m   Cash

3316222.2 Laura Finley

m   Allman

331623 Hoyt Poer Finley (26 Apr 1919-
lives Montgomery, AL
331624 Howard Finley (26 Apr 1919-26
Apr 1919)
33163 Howard <u>Heflin</u> Finley (1881-1947)
m Oma Yancy (-1950)
331631 Thomas Heflin Finley
m Lessie
331631.1 Frances Finley
33163.1 Aldora Finley (1884-)
m Thomas (Tom) Germany (1884-)
lived Plant City, FL
A Roy Germany
m Mamie Gaines
lives Ft. Meade, FL
B Nell Germany
m Roy Hicks
m Holsberry
lived Plant City, FL
C Joe Germany
m Willard Ford
lived Mulberry, FL
D Mary Elizabeth Germany (1911-1996)
m Nick DeVito (1912-1996)
lived Sarasota, FL
1 Sarah Anne Heart DeVito (1938-
m Jimmy Carlton Murray (1936-
a Mark Kevin Murray (1960-
m Surachanee (Nong) Bunnag
(1959-
1 Benmarong (Ben)
Bunnag Murray (94
2 Nick Menard DeVito (1940-
m Nancy Carole Alday (1942-
a Tamara (Tame) Autumn
DeVito (1961-
m Ian Ralph Stockfis
(1956-

             1 Niki Lei Stockfis (1982-
             m Joshua Timothy Griffin (1975-
             2 Kelsey Barbara Stockfis (1990-
             3 Brandon Alexander Stockfis (1992-
      b Nick Menard DeVito II (1967-
          m Susan Kerstan (1966-
        1 Dillon DeVito (1992-
        2 Dalton DeVito (1994-
        3 Danielle DeVito (1996-
      c Dini Lei DeVito (1971-
    E Sarah Fay Germany
    m John Hensley
    lived Plant City, FL
    F John Fred Germany
      m Mary Ellen Cook
      1 Sue Ellen Germany
          m Michael Lucas
             a Michael Lucas Jr
      2 John Germany
      3 Jan Fielder Germany (1960-
          m Mark Devane Gruetzmacher (1952-
        a Amy Fielder Gruetzmacher (1986-
        b Kate Ramsey Gruetzmacher (1987-
        c Mark Devane Gruetzmacher Jr (1990-
      4 Lindsey Germany
          m Jim Robbins
             a Jimmy Robbins
33163.2 Winnie Finley
m Lester Goodwin (-1973)
    A Martha Goodwin
    m R.J. Burton
    B June Goodwin

3317 James Taylor (Jim) Finley (28 Jan 1851-22 May 1933)
m 15 Oct 1874 Euphemia <u>Cumi</u> Mitchell (7 Jul 1854-
4 Apr 1941) in Lee Co., AL
bur Columbiana, Shelby Co., AL
3318 Samuel J. (Tink) Finley (c1856-2 Jan 1939)
m 30 Dec 1890 Pinkie Trammell in Lee Co., AL
lived in Loachapoka and Auburn in Lee Co., AL
first mayor of Loachapoka, AL
3318.1 Lucy A. Finley (c1859-6 Jan 1934)
m 18 Dec 1881 James A. Mullin in Lee Co., AL
   A Atticus Mullin (1894-1 Jul 1953)
   m 25 Jan 1913 Frankie Koerber
   newspaperman in Montgomery, AL
      1 Frances Mullin
      m Wakeman Lamar Jarrard
      2 Lucy Mullin
      m C.M. Burrows
         a James Christian Burrows
            1 Monica Hope Burrows
            2 Christian Beach Burrows (27 May 1979-
         b Joan Davidson Burrows
      3 Mary Mullin

Augustus H. Finley, oldest son of William and Elizabeth Haygood Finley, was born in Clarke (Oconee) County, Georgia. About 1830 he married Martha A. Powell, daughter of William Powell, who lived near the Finleys in Monroe County, Georgia and died in Marion County, Georgia in 1852 (Marion Co. WB A). While living in Monroe County Augustus Finley served as a Captain of Company 539 of the Georgia Militia from 22 Nov. 1827 until 22 Dec 1829.

The 1834 tax records of Monroe County, Georgia show Augustus owning 352 acres of land and three slaves. If you ignore the 500 acres his father William won in the land lottery, this means Augustus already had acquired more land than his father so it appears he was off to a fast start in life. He may have been helped by his father in law, who was a wealthy landowner.

By 1838, Augustus Finley had moved to Chambers County, Alabama where he was listed along with his father as a resident of Wickerville. Wickerville was located a few miles east of Lafayette. Shortly after 1840, he began buying land southwest of the crossroads at Freedonia.

Augustus amassed large holdings and undoubtedly became the wealthiest of our Finley ancestors in this country. He reached the zenith of his wealth in 1860 when he owned 1,550 acres of land valued at $5,000. He owned $500 worth of farm equipment, 7 horses, 7 asses and mules, 12 milch cows, 2 working oxen, 30 other cattle, 33 sheep, and 160 swine. The value of all his livestock was $2,500. That same year he had 100 bushels of wheat, 2,500 bushels of Indian corn, 80 bushels of oats, 40 bales of cotton, 75 pounds of wool, 100 bushels of peas and beans, 20 bushels of Irish potatoes, 300 bushels of sweet potatoes, 150 pounds of butter, 5 pounds of beeswax, 100 pounds of honey, and $900 worth of slaughtered meat. He also owned 31 slaves, which were his most valuable possessions.

During this period of time, he was a deacon of the Sharon Primitive Baptist Church, his name being mentioned as a representative of this church at a general meeting held in the Macedonia Church. In Lee County, he was a member of the Mt. Olive Primitive Baptist Church and on 30 April 1887 he and second wife Mary Ann transferred their letters to the Mt. Olive Primitive Baptist Church in Shelby County. His pastor at the first two churches was Rev. William Milton Mitchell, whose daughter married his son James.

The Civil War dealt him a severe economic blow. Of course he lost his slaves. It is very unlikely Chambers County ever repaid the $1,700 he loaned interest free to support the war effort. Land values dropped precipitously following the war as well and remained depressed for several decades. In spite of his losses, he remained a man of considerable wealth. He was able to loan money to make crops to other farmers in Lee County and he owned business property in Opelika as well as his farm land. We do not know if he ran a business in Opelika or simply rented out his building there.

It is likely all the oldest five sons of Augustus Finley served in the 14th Alabama regiment in the war. William P. Finley served in Company E (the Gilmer Grays). Henry H. Finley was a drummer in the 14th Infantry. This regiment fought in many battles including the Battle of Chickamauga. Augustus Clay Finley, too young to go to war at its onset, joined the 6th Alabama Cavalry when it was organized in 1864. Fortunately none of the sons lost their lives, but William P. Finley had a leg amputated during the war.

In 1866 Augustus moved to Lee County where he lived on the Macon County line southwest of Auburn and southeast of Loachapoka. Later he moved to a farm just south of the town limits of Opelika near the Mt. Olive Church. He owned two business buildings in Opelika. About 1887 at the age of 81, he moved with his younger set of children to Shelby County where he bought land near Columbiana on the road to Shelby. He died about a year later and is buried in the Columbiana cemetery. His will and estate papers are located in Shelby County Probate Final Record Book 2, pp. 151-165.

Mary Ann Hines had first married William G. Holt in 1838 in Troup County, Georgia. They had one daughter named Martha Jane Holt, called Mattie, born about 1840. William had died and left Mary Ann a widow. Perhaps there was friction between the two sets of children. Augustus had eight children and Mary Ann had only the one daughter. Mattie may have had difficulty coping with the more numerous children of Augustus. This is pure conjecture but for some reason in 1849 Martha Jane was placed under the guardianship of William Marsh, who lived in Freedonia. He had lived in Harris County, Georgia before moving to Chambers County. Most likely, William Marsh had married a sister of Mary Ann. Mary Ann Hines was the daughter of Thomas Hines who lived near William G. Holt in Troup County, Georgia in 1840. Thomas Hines is found in the Putnam County, Georgia censuses in 1820 and 1830. In the first decade of the nineteenth century Thomas lived in the southwestern corner of Greene County, Georgia. His wife was the daughter of Thomas Hightower of Greene County.

On 13 July 1858 Martha Jane Holt married William T. Smith, a dry goods merchant in Hickory Flat in Chambers County. Later in life as a widow she married the great grandfather of Dr. Robert Alexander Nunn of Loachapoka as his second wife. Dr. Nunn knew the Finleys personally and believed Mattie Smith was a half sister of James Taylor and Tink Finley. Orphans Court records of Chambers County lend support for this belief and there is no doubt his recollections are correct.

William P. Finley owned large tracts of land north of Freedonia in Chambers County. He was a representative to the Alabama Legislature in 1884-85. He and his wife are buried in the Freedonia Methodist Church cemetery. His son Emmett Finley practiced medicine in the Finley and Freedonia communities of Chambers County.

Henry H. Finley lived for a time in Troup County, Georgia. Ruth Crump, the historian of Chambers County, reported the Finleys and her Crowder ancestors were in a mill business together in Troup County and perhaps Henry was the one. In Chambers County he lived in the Ward's Mill community and was a postmaster at Wickerville. Late in life he lived with his daughter Leolia McCarley in the Buffaloe community. He is buried in the Emory Chapel Methodist Church cemetery.

Benjamen F. Finley seems to have lived with his grandmother and/ or his uncle A.B. Finley in the 1850 and 1860 censuses and helped them farm their land. He moved to Lee County where he lived near his father. He married widow Lucy Wright who is buried in the Elam Church cemetery in Macon County, Alabama. She was listed by herself in the 1900 census so he apparently died prior to that time. He seems not to have had any children.

John M. Finley is described in Civil War records as 5 feet, 8 ½ inches tall and of dark complexion. In 1888 he lived in Lisbon, Louisiana. Polk Finley says he was a preacher in Arkansas.

Polk also says Josiah C. Finley lived in Arkansas. He died about 1879 and his three children then lived with grandfather Augustus. His son Charles lived in Macon County, Alabama in 1888 and Y.J. Little of Macon County was appointed his guardian. Tink (Samuel J.) Finley was appointed guardian of children Frances and Josiah Austin and they likely moved with him to Lee County, Alabama.

Augustus Clay Finley lived in his grandmother Elizabeth Finley's house in 1850 and 1860. He moved from place to place in Chambers County and is buried in the Macedonia Primitive Baptist Church cemetery. His grandson Byron Bruce Finley was superintendent of schools in Clay County, Alabama. He was also a Primitive Baptist minister. B.B. Finley's son Wayne was a classmate of the author at the Medical College of Alabama. Wayne and his wife are both geneticists at the University of Alabama-Birmingham. B.B. Finley's brother Wyatt Horace Finley of Marietta, Georgia is currently clerk of the Macedonia Church and has custody of the church minutes.

Samuel J. (Tink) Finley moved with the family to Shelby County, Alabama. He bought the cemetery lot where the Finleys of Shelby County are buried, but after a short time he moved back to Lee County. He seems to have lived at times in Loachapoka and also at Auburn. He was the first mayor of Loachapoka when it was incorporated. He owned businesses, perhaps hardware stores, in Auburn, Loachapoka, and Notasulga. He married Pinkie Trammell, the daughter of John Young Trammell. They had no children.

Lucy Mullin's husband was a policeman in Birmingham and died at an early age, probably killed in the line of duty. Lucy was big and stout and jolly and was a big talker. She had severe arthritis in her knees and was unable to walk well. When she visited her brother in Shelby County she was carried around in a special wagon. Atticus Mullin was a brilliant student and earned a degree in civil engineering at Howard College (Samford U), the youngest graduate Howard had ever had at the time. However he lost a leg in a hunting accident and was unable to pursue his engineering career. Eventually he became a columnist for the Montgomery Advertiser, writing a column named "The Passing Throng." Lucy Burrows graduated from Judson College in 1937. Her husband is in the diplomatic corps. Their daughter, Joan Davidson Burrows, is a China scholar, speaking Mandarin Chinese, and formerly lived in Taiwan.

Chapter 9

JAMES TAYLOR FINLEY

3317 James Taylor Finley (28 Jan 1851-22 May 1933)
m 15 Oct 1874 Euphemia <u>Cumi</u> Mitchell (7 Jul 1854-8 Apr 1941)
bur Columbiana, AL cemetery
  33171 Charlie Lee Finley (16 Aug 1875-28 Aug 1968)
  m 15 Mar 1903 Elizabeth Dela Easley (9 Sep 1886-23 May 1948)
  bur Drivers Cemetery, Teague, TX
    331710.1 Opal Mae Finley (27 Mar 1905-
    m 24 Dec 1928 Jacob Petty (21 May 1908-28 Mar 1960) lives Dunn, TX
      A Roy Alfred Petty (24 Jan 1930-
      m Margaret Welch
      m Freda
      lives Westbrook, TX
        1 Roy Allen Petty
        m Karen
        2 Carol Ann Petty
        m Richard Northrip
        lives Taft, CA

        a Kimberly Diana Northrip (18 Oct
        1977-
    3 Bobby Lee Petty
    4 David Petty
    5 Jimmy Petty
    6 Mike Petty
B Janie Pearl Petty (16 Jan 1932-
m 2 Jan 1948 Jack Wm Breen (2 Sep 1926-
Sep 1976)
m Louis Dlouhy (26 Apr 1921-
lives Crosby, TX
    1 Ralph William Breen (12 May 1941-
    m 9 Jun 1978 Carol Vrana Flynn
    lives Channelview, TX
        a Jake Wesley Breen (14 Jul 1979-
    2 Steve Howard Breen (15 Jul 1950-
    m 13 Dec 1969 Glenda Gale Pennon
    lives Channelview, TX
        a Carrie Ann Breen (24 Aug 1971-
        b Steve Breen Jr. (3 Jan 1976-
        c Misty Michelle Breen (9 Sep
        1978-
    3 Mary Elizabeth Breen (12 Jul 1971-
    m Dec 1967 Tony Hutman
        a Donna Jean Hutman
    4 Cynthia Jane Dlouhy (29 Aug 1960-
    lives Crosby, TX
C Hazel Joe Petty (20 Dec 1936-
m Alton E. Smith
lives Dunn, TX
    1 Jeffery Leroy Smith (28 Jan 1955-
D Ona Mozell Petty (11 Apr 1940-
m Bobby Robinson (9 Nov 1936-
lives Pecos, TX
    1 Kathy Robinson
    m Royce Overton
    2 Judy Robinson
    3 James Lynn Robinson
    4 Donna Jean Robinson

E Elizabeth Inez Petty (1 Aug 1943-
m 18 Jul 1961 Shelby Ray Gilbert (6 Jan 1943-
Lives Channelview, TX
   1 Jerry Wayne Gilbert (15 Mar 1963-
   2 Shari Ladine Gilbert (14 Apr 1971-
331710.2 Annie Lucille Finley (27 Sep 1907-
m 22 Jul 1923 Clark Walthall (29 Mar 1902-
lives Houston, TX
  A Etta Mae Walthall (26 Apr 1924-
m 14 May 1944 Fred John Buckner (12 Dec 1924-
lives Houston, TX
   1 Jerry Wayne Buckner (3 Sep 1946-
   m 7 Apr 1968 Linda Dianna Powledge
   lives Pasadena, TX
      a Steven Wayne Buckner (8 Jul 1969-
      b Lori Lynn Buckner (22 Aug 1972-
   2 Susan Denice Buckner (24 Nov 1959-
  B Lester Ray Walthall (29 Jan 1926-
m 31 May 1947 Juanita Crawford (4 Jun 1926-
lives Baytown, TX
   1 Michall Ray Walthall (8 Oct 1950-
      a Michall Glen Walthall (21 Jan 1966-
   2 Miles Curtis Walthall (19 Jan 1954-
      a Miles Chap Walthall (19 Oct 1970-
  C Opal Fay Walthall (21 Feb 1928-
m 6 May 1946 Ira Carlton Jackson (1930-1952)
m 6 Jan 1953 Lonnie Ray Taylor
lives Richmond, TX
   1 Perry Michael Taylor (7 Oct 1959-

   a Perry Michael Taylor Jr. (16 Sep 1978-
D Lizzie Charlene Walthall (12 Oct 1932-
m 6 Dec 1947 Jasper Prince Finney (10 Jun 1924-
lives Houston, TX
  1 James Paul Finney (22 Jul 1953-
  m 21 Mar 1978 Betty Jo Allen (7 Jul 1956-
  lives Houston, TX
   a James Paul Finney Jr. (6 Feb 1979-
  2 Pamela Loucele Finney (29 Jul 1956-
  m 22 Nov 1974 Gary Mack Weaver (22 Sep 1951-
  lives Houston, TX
E James Clark Walthall (13 Jan 1942-
m 30 May 1963 Wanda Mae Hice (13 Sep 1945-
lives Houston, TX
  1 Carl Wayne Walthall (1 Jul 1964-
331710.3 Beatrice Cumi Finley (15 Feb 1910-
m 1 Jan 1929 William Andy Cartwright (- 1945)
lives Teague, TX
  A William Alvin Cartwright (30 Nov 1929-
  m Erma Lee Connell
  lives Teague, TX
   1 Debra Cartwright (10 Nov 1959-
   2 Cynthia Cartwright (21 Nov 1961-
   3 Sandra Cartwright (2 Nov 1963-
   4 Angela Cartwright (31 Oct 1969-
  B Jimmie Louise Cartwright (30 May 1931-
  m Gene Nance

lives Ganada, TX
    1 **Larry Ray Nance** (11 Feb 1952-
    a **Amanda Marie Nance**
    2 **Carol Ann Nance** (10 Oct 1956-
    m Fowler
        a **Brenda Fowler** (25 Jan 1975-
        b **Jamie Louise Fowler** (17 May
        1979-
C **Frances Cartwright** (22 Nov 1940-
m Donald Martin
lives Dallas, TX
    1 **Rhonda Martin** (7 Sep 1963-
    2 **Ronald Martin** (28 Dec 1964-
    3 **Robert Martin** (11 Nov 1973-
331711 Hershel Marvin Finley (18 Jan
1912-
m 31 Oct 1936 Margaret Ray
lives Teague, TX
    3317111 Charles Ray Finley (17 Sep
    1937-
    m Dorothy Banneau
    lives Missouri City, TX
        33171110.1 Michelle Finley (10 Mar
        1962-
        33171111 Mark Edward Finley (17 Jan
        1964-
        33171112 Charles Anthony Finley (30
        Jun 1966-
    3317111.1 Susan Elizabeth Finley (29
    Mar 1952-
    m 17 Mar 1977 Bob Blackmon
    lives Friendswood, TX
331712 Vernon Lee Finley (14 Feb 1914-
m 25 Apr 1936 Margaret Terry (3 Oct 1920-
lives Teague, TX
    3317121 Henry Lee Finley (4 Dec 1939-
    m 21 Sep 1964 Marylyn Beene
    lives Whitney, TX

3317122 **Willie Frank Finley** (25 Dec 1941-
m 7 Feb 1969 Linda Neal
lives Whitney, TX

> 33171221 **Willie Frank Finley Jr.** (7 May 1971-
> 33171221.1 **Meloni Finley** (7 Oct 1975-

3317123 **Charles Kenneth Finley** (12 Feb 1944-
m 4 Oct 1966 Ruth Isbell
lives Coolidge, TX

> 33171231 **Charles Kenneth Finley Jr** (2 Oct 1967
> 33171232 **Danny Finley** (21 Jun 1969-
> 33171232.1 **Melinda Finley** (12 Apr 1973-

3317124 **John Allen Finley** (18 Apr 1946-
m 1967 Diann Johnson
lives Teague, TX

> 33171240.1 **Lynda Finley** (18 Oct 1968-

3317124.1 **Catherine Elizabeth Finley** (10 Oct 1948-
m 14 Oct 1967 K.W. Oliver
lives Wortham, TX

> A **April Rebecca Oliver** (22 Apr 1975-

3317125 **Richard Wayne Finley** (22 Jan 1959-
lives Teague, TX

331712.1 **Vivian Allene Finley** (2 Mar 1917-
m Bill Burns
lives Ladonia, TX

331712.2 **Dorothy Mozell Finley** (8 Jan 1919-4 Jun 1922)

331713 **James Taylor Finley** (31 Dec 1920-
m 1945 Lorene Miller

m 16 Jul 1960 Vickie Elizabeth Brooks
lives Fort Worth, TX

3317131 James Donald Finley (12 Feb 1946-

33171310.1 Angia Mashell Finley (11 Oct 1976-

3317131.1 Elizabeth Maxine Finley (31 Aug 1947-

m Ronnie Davis

A Darrell Wayne Davis (7 Feb 1969-

B Laura Davis (26 Feb 1973-

3317132 David Taylor Finley (18 Mar 1961-

3317132.1 Vickie Marlene Finley (22 Aug 1963-

3317132.2 Dawn Renia Finley (8 Apr 1970-

331714 John Allen Finley (9 Jul 1923-11 Dec 1944)

331714.1 Mary Bell Finley (26 Jul 1925-

m 16 Feb 1946 Jesse Lee Smith
m 22 Jul 1974 Grayson Lee White
lives Angleton, TX

A David Lester Smith (11 Jan 1947-

m 11 Feb 1972 Marcia Davis

B Gene Louis Smith (14 Aug 1950-

m 10 Feb 1977 Mary Neeala Cornelius

1 Amber Collene Smith (4 Jun 1979-

331714.2 Thelma Finley (29 Jun 1928-1937)

331714.3 Lavern Finley (31 Dec 1929-1 Jan 1930)

33172 William Everette Finley (7 May 1877-13 Dec 1962)

m 20 Nov 1904 Nora Clemantine Wingard (1887-1972)
bur Columbiana, AL Cemetery

33173 Augustus <u>Bernard</u> Finley (18 Sep 1878-24 Jan 1940)

m 30 Nov 1902 Essie Estha Branch (26 Sep 1882-1936)
bur Columbiana, AL cemetery

331731 Virgil Clay Finley (28 Oct 1905-
m 11 Aug 1940 Annie Marie Chemell Tillman (1905-

331732 Howard Finley (9 Jan 1908-11 Apr 1972)
m 24 Dec 1931 Zora Mae Hale (11 Jan 1912-2002)

3317320.1 Doris Elizabeth Finley (28 Oct 1932-
m 6 Jan 1951 Earskine Jr. Hall (15 Aug 1932-

A Ricky Lane Hall (22 May 1953-
m 1970 Debbie Marie Berry
m Renee Elizabeth Miller (17 May 1952-

1 Genia Marie Hall (13 Dec 1971-
2 Richard Jeremiah Hall (10 Jul 1978-

3317320.2 Essie Ann Finley (28 Apr 1938-
m 26 May 1956 William Monroe Wood Jr.

A Teresa Diann Wood (7 Jan 1958-
m 17 May 1980 Michael Smiley (27 Aug 1955-

B William Michael Wood (15 Jul 1959-

3317321 David Hoyt Finley (2 Nov 1939-
m 6 Nov 1959 Dorothy Templin (28 Jul 1940-

33173211 David Lane Finley (25 Sep 1963-

33173211.1 Angie Renee Finley (11 Mar 1966-

3317322 Howard Finley Jr. (2 Oct 1943-
m 21 Feb 1964 Judy Lynn Dennison (4 Apr 1946-
m 21 Mar 1980 Peggy Beaty Kelley

33173220.1 Rachell Lynn Finley (5 Aug 1967-

33173221 Clayton Douglas Finley

331732.1 Elvie Finley (19 Oct 1910-
m Howard Hayes, DVM
lives Hueytown, AL

A Charles Edgar Hayes (14 Oct 1935-
m 27 Nov 1957 Viola Beard (17 May 1935-
m Barbara Carol Breland (8 Jan 1939-
lives Mobile, AL

   1 **Malinda Carol Hayes** (30 Jan 1959-
m 1 Sep 1979 Greg Kilgore

   2 **Donna Lynn Hayes** (19 Aug 1961-

   3 **Charles Howard Hayes** (19 Jan 1964-

   4 **Jennifer Ann Hayes** (17 Apr 1970-

   5 **Rickie Breland** (20 Jul 1956-

   6 **Eddie Breland** (15 Dec 1958-

   7 **Dwaylah Breland** (24 Sep 1960-

   8 **Bryan Breland** (21 Apr 1965-

   9 **Charles Edgar Walker Hayes** (27 Dec 1979-

B Paul Jackson Hayes (12 Oct 1937-
m 21 Jul 1962 Marilyn Gail Dowdy (17 Nov 1939-

   1 **David Paul Hayes** (28 Apr 1963-

   2 **Karen Gail Hayes** (5 Dec 1968-

   3 **Natalie Marilyn Hayes** (20 Sep 1972-

C Martha Ann Hayes (8 Mar 1939-
m 15 Jul 1972 Robert McLean Livingston (1935-

   1 **Andrew Howard Livingston** (5 May 1976-

   2 **Ann Elizabeth Livingston** (26 Dec 1973-

D William Finley Hayes (15 Nov 1943-
m 1 Jun 1963 Brenda Joyce Waldrop (10 Apr 1945-

   1 **Laurie Ann Hayes** (16 Apr 1964-

  2 **Christie Lee Hayes** (18 Jun 1968-
  3 **William Brian Hayes** (19 May 1973-
331733 Dewey Finley (10 Dec 1912-13 Aug 1942)
m Aug 1940 Vivian Haskew (28 Jan 1912-
 3317331 James Dewey Finley (3 Nov 1941-28 Oct 1963)
331733.1 Maxine Cumi Finley (26 Apr 1918-
331733.2 Willie Mae Finley (9 Aug 1922-
m 15 May 1943 William Harold Baxley Jr.(4 Oct 1917-
 A Gail Joyce Baxley (14 Jun 1947-
 m 13 Nov 1969 Michael Wm Brannon (4 Nov 1944-
  1 **Brandy Marie Brannon** (8 Mar 1976-
  2 **Michele Lea Brannon**
 B William Harold Baxley III (30 Mar 1952-
331733.2 Mary Nell Finley (9 Dec 1923-
m 21 Mar 1948 Siggle Sylvester Shaw Jr.(1921-1978)
 A Siggle Sylvester Shaw III (21 Aug 1949-
 m May 1972 Linda Louise Rudlinger (12 Jun 1948-
  1 **Siggle Sylvester Shaw IV** (2 Apr 1974-1974)
  2 **Benjamin Jason Shaw** (23 Aug 1975-
  3 **Alexander Jacob Shaw** (9 Mar 1978-
 B Larry Bernard Shaw (7 Dec 1951-
  1 **Jason Bernard Shaw** (13 Jul 1980-
 C Dewey Clifford Shaw (10 Mar 1959-
33173.1 Mary Cumi Finley (1882-)
m Henry Latham
lived Docena, AL - ni
33173.2 Annie Lucy Finley (1885-)
m John Rhodes
lived Tampa, FL - ni

33173.3 **Emma E. Finley** (6 Feb 1885-11 Nov 1890)

33174 **James Taylor Finley Jr.** (1889- May 1971)

m Althea Inez Angle

bur Olive Branch Church cemetery, Owassa, AL

    331741 James Taylor Finley III (22 Jul 1924-)

    m Chesteen Robinson (22 Jul 1927-

    d Chesley Robinson

    bur Olive Branch Church Cemetery, Owassa, AL

        3317410.1 Janet Kay Finley (10 Jan 1953-

        m Clifford E. Evans

            A Kustin Taylor Evans (30 Sep 1982-

            B Ashley Nicole Evans (18 May 1989-

        3317411 James Alonzo Finley (8 Sep 1956-

            33174111 James Daniel Finley (19 Jan 1984-

33174.1 Nannie Lois Finley (1890-1894)

Jim Finley, oldest of the children of Augustus H. Finley and Mary Ann Hines Holt, was born in Chambers County, Alabama. Shortly after the Civil War, the family moved to Lee County to the area south of Auburn and Loachapoka adjacent to the Macon County line where I-85 crosses it. Choctofaula Creek coursed through the middle of their land and we can imagine the children refreshed themselves in its cool waters. In 1868 Jim attended school for 34 days at Elam School, where H.H. Hargrove was his teacher. His brother Tink attended for 51 days and sister Lucy attended 145 days that year. Elam School was located on highway 29 just across the line in Macon County. A small cemetery is all that is left to mark the spot of the Elam Church which was just across the road from the school.

The Finleys attended Mount Olive Primitive Baptist Church. They had become acquainted with the pastor, William Milton Mitchell, when he had earlier pastored the Sharon Church in Chambers County. Jim's father had been a deacon of the Sharon Church. Jim won the heart of the preacher's daughter Cumi.

It seems Jim farmed the land south of Auburn and Loachapoka after his father moved nearer the church and adjacent to the Opelika City limits. Living next door in 1880 were families of blacks named Finley who were likely former slaves of his father. In 1880 Jim farmed 290 acres of land worth $2,000. He had $100 worth of farm implements. He had 5 horses, 3 milch cows, 9 other cattle, and 38 swine with a total value of his livestock set at $500. He grew 37 bushels of wheat on 10 acres, 300 bushels of Indian corn on 30 acres, 175 bushels of oats on 35 acres, 17 bales of cotton on 37 acres, and 100 bushels of sweet potatoes on 1 acre. He had 3 calves dropped in 1880. In that year he had $50 worth of repairs to his buildings and spent $75 for fertilizer. He paid $250 in wages and had a farm production of $1,100.

In 1887 Jim moved to Shelby County where he bought 118 acres of land about two miles west of Columbiana for $750. Two acres of this tract of land had previously been given to the Mount Olive Primitive Baptist Church, which was just around a curve in the road from his house. Will Finley often told his children how he drove the cows behind the wagon for this move and how tired he became. He also told of carrying logs to Wilsonville to have them sawed into lumber and of bringing the lumber back to build the house. The foundations of this house can still be located about 100 yards northeast of the junction of county roads 70 and 74. In the Spring the ground is covered with buttercups in bloom, which Cumi originally planted.

The house had two stories. Upstairs was one large room where the boys slept and downstairs the house was separated by a hall from front to back. There was a porch all the way across the front with vines planted on a frame at one end to shield the sun. The house also had two other porches. On one side of the hall was the living room, dining room, and kitchen. On the other side of the hall were the bedrooms for the girls and the parents. The mules were kept in a barn across the road from the house and there was a spring on that side of the road which provided water. The cows were kept in a barn on the same side of the road as the house. There was a buggy shed near the house and probably two or three other small buildings. A tall thin tree still stands at the edge of the original roadbed which was planted by the Finleys. In the corner of the yard stood a Black Walnut tree which was recently cut down. Some of the walnuts were still lying on the ground the day I was there. The house and barns were always neat and the tools were always in place. Jim Finley sold this land in 1926 for $1,100.

As old age approached and the children had left home, the Finleys moved to the Dargen Community. Their farm was immediately adjacent to the present intersection of Highway I-65 and US 31 on the southeastern side. A recently built Holiday Inn Express is either located on land they owned or very close to it. Here they lived next to their son Bernard. Highway 31, which was being paved at the time, ran in front of the house. It was the first paved road in Shelby County. This house had a parlor, dining room, kitchen, two bedrooms, and a screened-in porch, or "sleeping porch" across the back. Within the walls of the sleeping porch was a cistern. A pear tree still bears fruit next to where the house stood, although the fruit is stunted from lack of cultivation. Jim Finley owned a pretty red horse and a rubber-tired buggy. When riding down the pavement of the highway he would sometimes say "Rubber-tired buggy and a cushioned seat, all you hear is the horse's feet." Sometimes he rode to Calera, delivering eggs and butter to customers along the way. He hung the eggs, milk, and butter on ropes in the cistern for refrigeration.

Cumi Finley told Elvie Hayes that Jim was a Methodist in the early days of their marriage. He did not join the Primitive Baptist Church until after they had married. On 6 August 1887 James T. and Euphemia C. Finley presented letters of dismission from the Mt. Olive Primitive Baptist Church in Lee County and joined the Mt. Olive Church in Shelby County. On Saturday before the first Sunday in March, 1911, J.T. was ordained a deacon of the church. He also served as clerk pro tem, assistant clerk, and clerk. They always went to the meetings on first Saturdays and Sundays and Jim always sat on the front bench. Cumi of course sat across the aisle with the other ladies. Jim's favorite song was "I'm Long Time Traveling Here Below." He made sure this song was sung at every meeting. B.B. Finley remembered meeting him at a Primitive Baptist meeting in the Wetumpka Association. The Finleys used to get out blankets and made beds and pallets in the barns for people who came to church meetings and lived too far away to return home at night. (Primitive Baptists commonly met once a month and met all weekend rather than just on Sunday.) Cumi would bake a sack of flour for breakfast in order to feed all the people who were staying. The Finleys always swept out the church building and got the church ready for meetings.

Jim Finley is remembered as a good Christian man and a hard worker. He was known to be frugal, a Finley trademark. He was respected in the community and owned stock in and was a director of Columbiana Savings Bank. He was probably one of the very few Republicans in Shelby County. Even though he was a director of the bank, Elvie Hayes remembers that on one occasion he had to declare bankruptcy. She remembers him hiding the farm machinery from the creditors who came looking for the assets of his estate. It may be that her memory is clouded and what she remembers is the time Will Finley lost his farm following a flood. Perhaps he moved some of his equipment to his father's farm in order to hide it from creditors.

Jim Finley died at the age of 82. He had never failed to make a crop. He had been chopping cotton on the morning of his death. At the lunch table he took a cramp in his legs, something that occurred to him often.

This inclination to have leg cramps apparently was handed down to his son Will and to others of his descendants. On this occasion he jumped up and walked from room to room, with Cumi following with a liniment bottle trying to rub his legs. When he got to the back room, or perhaps the screened-in porch, he lay down and in a few minutes he was dead. The doctor said he died of "apoplexy of the brain" (a stroke). His funeral service was held at the Mt. Olive Primitive Baptist Church and he was buried beside his father and mother in the Columbiana cemetery.

According to an article in the Columbiana paper, the service was conducted by his pastor, Rev. Mr. Streetman assisted by Elder Houk of Birmingham. The following quote is taken from the article, "Many sincere tributes were paid to Mr. Finley by his friends and neighbors. One man who had lived by him for many years said that he had never known a better neighbor than Mr. Finley was. Another friend who had been intimately associated with him in a business way, said 'Mr. Finley was a man without prejudice. He settled every issue from the standpoint of right and wrong. When he made up his mind that a thing was right he stood by it without compromise.'"

Cumi Mitchell Finley is remembered as "a mighty sweet grandmother." All the grandchildren loved to stay with her. She was a number one cook and housekeeper. Lucille Merrell remembered that a salesman would arrange his route so he could spend the night at her house. He said whenever he knocked at her door, he could always know that she would have a broom, dustcloth, or something similar in her hands because she was always cleaning the house. Her house always smelled like spices. She was tall and slim with a big frame and was several inches taller than Jim. She wore long, straight, high-necked dresses. She always referred to Jim as "Mr. Finley." When riding in the buggy she would sometimes say, "There is a hole in my side of the road, Mr. Finley." Perhaps she was one of the earliest backseat drivers. She always referred to the porches of the house as verandas. In the morning she drank hot water while others were drinking coffee. Her biscuits were first-rate. She had a hop vine in the garden, from which she made her own yeast. She would boil the leaves and mix them with water and flour and perhaps other ingredients to make a loaf of bread. Her boys would come to the table and say, "Thank you for the hop bread, butter, and syrup." She cooked on a wood stove known as a Home Comfort which had a warming closet on top. Catherine Vardaman remembered she always had double crust, green apple pies ready to eat. Elvie Hayes remembers she always had cookies baked. When the grandchildren were visiting, she always put them to work.

Lucille Merrell shared this recipe for blackberry jam cake which was handed down to her from Cumi.
"1 cup sugar
½ cup butter
1 cup jam (blackberry)
3 eggs
1/4 teaspoon each of cloves, cinnaman, and spice
1 ½ cup plain flour

1 teaspoon soda & salt (have oven hot)
2 nine inch greased cake pans
bake 30 minutes at 350

Icing
1 cup sugar
½ cup S milk
butter size of walnut
boil 20 minutes or till forms a soft ball when dropped in cold water
stack with icing between layers and on top and sides."

Elvie Hayes thinks Cumi had typhoid fever in middle life and was sick for a long time. Afterwards she never seemed to be very strong. She remembers Jim would have to do the heavier work around the house. He would draw the water and carry it into the house and take care of other household chores that required strength.

Elvie also remembers Jim and Cumi spoiled their children. When her Aunt Annie was a child, she once said, "I can't eat, we don't have any syrup." Jim went to Columbiana in the buggy to get some syrup. Myrtle Schrock loved to eat sausage, but her grandmother would let her have only one piece. One time she stayed with her grandfather while Cumi was away for a couple of days. They ate all the sausage they wanted. When Cumi returned, she noticed the sausage was gone and made a remark about it. Jim said nothing but looked at Myrtle and winked.

I can find no records in the Shelby County courthouse of the settlement of the estate of

James Finley. Apparently everything was left to the widow and the estate was not settled until after her death. The settlement of her estate is located in Shelby County Probate Final Record Book 12, p. 341. Will Finley served as administrator. The total amount of the estate was less than $4,000.

Oldest son Charlie Lee Finley moved to Texas where he lived all his adult life. He married after arriving in Texas, and his wife would never accompany him back to Alabama, apparently being afraid he would not return to Texas if she did. I remember him coming to visit on one occasion and he limped and walked with a cane. He apparently had broken his leg in his youth and it had shortened in the healing process. All the family members remember he was a big talker, as were his brothers. It was difficult for anyone else to say anything when two of them were together.

Bernard Finley lived all his life in Shelby County. He owned a farm in the Dargen Community next to where his father later moved. Bernard Finley was the only one of the children who was tall like his mother. He was several inches taller than his brothers. His son Howard lived in the Saginaw Community of Shelby County. His daughter Elvie moved in with her grandmother after her grandfather's death and it was during this time she was told many of the stories which she has in turn shared with the author.

Taylor Finley moved to Conecuh County about 1911. He traveled over Conecuh County in a wagon selling patent medicines. He was known throughout the county as Doc Finley. During

World War I, his vocation earned him a spot in the medical corps. He lived in Owassa, next to where his son James later lived.

The following is the genealogy of the Mitchell family:

Henry Mitchell (c1768-22 Nov 1843)
m Mary Ann (22 Dec 1770-14 Sep 1810)
   11 James Mitchell (1793-1867)
   m Margaret McCammon (1794-1850)
   m Theresa White (13 Feb 1803-8 Jun 1879)
   12? John Mitchell

According to family historians, Henry Mitchell was born in Virginia. By 1800 he had settled in Chester District, South Carolina. Other Mitchells who lived in Chester District in 1800 who may have been old enough to have been Henry's father were James, Isaiah, and Elias. According to census information, Henry had three sons born between 1794-1800 and three born between 1800-10. He had five daughters, one born before 1794. We have to assume the John Mitchell who lived near James in Macon County, Alabama in 1840 was one of the sons of Henry Mitchell.

Henry and Mary Ann Mitchell are both buried in the Smith's Chapel Methodist Episcopal Church Cemetery which is located three or four miles north of the city of Chester. In <u>Tombstone Records of Chester County, South Carolina and Vicinity</u>, Louise Kelly Crowder copied the following inscription from Henry Mitchell's tombstone in 1957, "Died November 22, 1843 in his 76th year." Later she returned to the cemetery and reported his tombstone was missing.

1 James Mitchell (1793-1867)
m Margaret McCammon (1794-1850)
m Theresa White (13 Feb 1803-8 Jun 1879)
  11 William Milton Mitchell (10 Jan 1819-26 Feb 1901)
  m 2 Jun 1842 Mary E. Taylor (4 Aug 1826-2 Jun 1903)
  11.1 Mrs. Josiah Payne
  11.2 Mrs. Millege Towles
  11.3 Mrs. F.M. Taylor
  12 John Henry Mitchell
  13 Hardy Mitchell
  14 Watson Mitchell

Most of the information on James Mitchell comes from Alabama Historical Quarterly, vol. 15, no. 2, pp. 232-8. The quotes in this section of the history come from this magazine. This volume of the Quarterly is a reprint of articles which originally were printed in the Opelika Times, 1883-1885, written by the Rev.F.L. Cherry under the pen name "Okosee." Rev. Cherry knew James Mitchell and his son William Milton personally. He mentions a footwashing ceremony which he witnessed in which James and William were participants. Cherry was deeply affected by William when he asked his father if he were worthy to wash his feet.

James Mitchell was born in Chester District, South Carolina in 1793. At 16 years of age he was "bound out" as an apprentice to learn the carpenter's and millwright's trade under Captain McCammon. There was a William Cammon listed near Henry Mitchell in the 1800 census and this is probably the Captain McCammon mentioned by Rev. Cherry. James performed his duties so well he was able to win the affection of Margaret McCammon, the captain's sister. They moved to Troup County, Georgia about 1833, where James built mills about ten miles from the city of La Grange. The mills burned in 1837 and James sold his land and moved in an oxcart to Macon County, Alabama. He again built mills on Chewacla Creek, grinding corn and wheat. He also built a sawmill and is said to have cut millions of feet of lumber. Most of the early buildings of Auburn and Opelika are said to have been built from lumber from his sawmill.

It seems the first member of the family to join the church was William Milton. Margaret wanted to join at the same time, but James forbade her to be baptized. He made her put her baptism off for one month. Then when she was baptized, he joined the church also. He became a steadfast member of the Mount Olive Primitive Baptist Church and was elected a deacon of this church. In 1852 he built the present church building, which is located about four miles south of Opelika on the Society Hill Road.

James Mitchell later suffered a series of financial disasters, but he retained his integrity and the confidence of the people through it all. "He was a quiet man but it was an energetic quietude, saying comparatively little, yet, that little well."

James and his second wife are buried in the Mount Olive Church Cemetery. There is also a stone erected in memory of Margaret McCammon Mitchell but her grave is in the original church cemetery which is located about two miles south of the present church building on a hilltop. Margaret was the mother of all the children. It is said that those of the family with red hair got it from her.

Rev. Cherry states James and Margaret had eight children with one dying in infancy. He then listed the first five which appear in the list above. Family members have told me there was another son named Watson who left on horseback for Texas and had not been heard of since, until recently when one of his descendants came back to the Mitchell family reunion. Mrs. Josiah Payne is said to be the grandmother of Mr. Warren Payne of Auburn, Alabama and great grandmother of Mr. Howard A. Payne of Opelika at the time of Rev. Cherry's writing. Mrs. F.M. Taylor is said to have died after only one month of marriage. John Henry Mitchell made a trip to Mississippi and died there before the Civil War. Hardy Mitchell fought and died in the war.

The 1850 census of Macon County lists the children of James Mitchell still living at home as Sarah, Amanda, Susannah, Robert, and William. Apparently Robert and William were the other names of Hardy and Watson.

11 William Milton Mitchell (10 Jan 1819-26 Feb 1901)
m 2 Jun 1842 Mary E. Taylor (4 Aug 1826-2 Jun 1903)
>**110.1 Nancy Lucinda Mitchell (17 Mar 1843-27 Feb 1924)**
>m James T. Puckett (26 Mar 1836-21 Jul 1916)
>**111 John M. Mitchell (c1845-16 May 1863)**

111.Emily Hester Mitchell (23 Nov 1846-8 Aug 1918)

m John Hanson

112 Jessie G. Mitchell (16 Dec 1849-29 Dec 1914)

113 Gira G. Mitchell Sr. (1 Sep 1851-30 Dec 1943)

m Mary Ann   (7 Aug 1860-16 Aug 1911)

113.1 Euphemia <u>Cumi</u> Mitchell (7 Jul 1854-8 Apr 1941)

m 15 Oct 1874 James Taylor Finley (28 Jan 1851-22 May 1933)

113.2 Janie Mitchell (15 Oct 1856-15 Dec 1936)

m Jim Moore

114 Ira Brown Mitchell (23 Dec 1858-10 Jun 1927)

m Virginia Key (1862-1943)

115 William Morgan Mitchell (16 Aug 1861-4 Oct 1919)

m Naomi Key

116 Charles Francis Mitchell (21 Jan 1866-12 Mar 1923)

117 Virgil David Mitchell (9 Mar 1870-20 Mar 1939)

William Milton Mitchell was born in Chester District, South Carolina and moved with the family to the Chewacla Creek neighborhood of what is now Lee County, Alabama. As a young man he was crushed when a load of logs shifted in the wagon and he injured his back. Another account says he hurt his back lifting when he was 15 years old. Either way he suffered from back pain all his life. He was unable to preach for about five years from 1850 to 1854. In old age and perhaps before he walked with a cane. This cane was handed down to Cumi

Finley and eventually to Lucille Merrell who gave it to the author.

William taught school in Chewacla from 1841 to 1843. One of his pupils was the wife of Rev. Cherry. He was baptized in 1842 and was one of the original six members who organized the Mount Olive Primitive Baptist Church in 1843. On the fourth Sunday of June 1843, he preached his first sermon and was licensed as a minister of the gospel. He was ordained in 1845 and served several Primitive Baptist churches in Chambers County in the 1840's - Enon, Macedonia, Canaan, and Sharon. At Sharon he became acquainted with the Finleys who were members of that church. He served alternately as clerk or moderator of the Beulah Primitive Baptist Association for twenty years.

In 1850 he had 45 acres of improved land and 55 acres of unimproved land valued at $500. He owned 2 horses, 2 milch cows, 3 other cattle, and 13 swine valued all together at $225. He had 250 bushels of Indian corn, 40 bushels of oats, 1 bale of cotton, 20 bushels of sweet potatoes, 55 pounds of butter, and $50 worth of slaughtered meat.

Sometime after 1850 he returned to the Chewacla neighborhood and became pastor of the Mt. Olive Primitive Baptist Church. Although he was subject to an annual recall, he served as pastor of this church for over 50 years. As one of descendants said, "For him to serve 50 years in a Primitive Baptist church, he had to be a good man." Today a large picture of Elder Mitchell hangs on the wall of the room behind the auditorium of the church. Elder

Mitchell had a strong influence in the Chewacla neighborhood but he also was well known in Primitive Baptist circles throughout the country. Elder Sylvester Hassell in History of the Church of God, From the Creation to A.D. 1885 says "His ministry and usefulness have abounded to a very considerable extent down to the present period. He has traveled in a number of States and made numerous personal acquaintances; his preaching is much approved by brethren in general, and his able communications for Baptist periodicals for a number of years have been both comforting and instructive to the household of faith...He has never been connected with any religious sect or institution except the Primitive Baptists, and never had a desire to be, either from principle or curiosity. He has now for several years been associate editor (with Elder J.R. Respess of Butler, Taylor County, Ga.) of the 'Gospel Messenger.' The Primitive Baptists have no more esteemed minister or writer in the United States than Elder Mitchell." He became associate editor of the Gospel Messenger in 1881. Rev.B.B. Finley of Lineville, Alabama said he was known as the father of Primitive Baptists in Texas. He is said to have taken preaching trips to eleven other states. His writings are still widely read by Primitive Baptists. G.W. Stewart in The Primitive Pathway, It's Mile-posts and Sign-boards quotes his defense of numerous Primitive Baptist doctrines.

William Milton Mitchell built a house on the Society Hill Road about a mile north of the Mt. Olive Church in the early 1850's, a house which still stands. Some of the plaster has fallen from the chimneys, revealing the flat creek-bottom rocks it was built with. He farmed 280 acres of land valued at $2200 in 1880. On one occasion the family had company for dinner. The adults had finished eating their fried chicken and the men were sitting around the table talking. The children were waiting impatiently in the kitchen for their chance at the chicken. At the urging of the other children, Ira cracked the door and said in a loud voice, "I bet nobody at that table is as hungry as I am." Everyone expected Ira to receive a severe reprimand, but the adults only took the hint and moved to the parlor so the children could eat.

William Milton was a very stern man and did not talk to his children often. Elizabeth Ingram remembered her father did not feel free to talk with him.

When the Yankees came through Opelika in 1864, the Mitchells sent Jesse down the road with the horses to hide them in the woods. However as Jesse was making his way he ran into the yanks who relieved him of his burden. The Yankees also availed themselves of the Mitchell's hospitality and ate at their table. They were not very gracious and were not well thought of by the Mitchells.

G.W. Stewart quotes Elder Mitchell as saying, "I have always been poor, and have raised a family of ten children on a little farm. I have suffered many severe misfortunes, both physically and pecuniarily, and am never without pain. But I have always lived within my income; sometimes my entire store account has only amounted to ten dollars a year."

William M. and Mary E. Mitchell are both buried in the Mt. Olive Cemetery.

Mary E. Mitchell was the daughter of Jesse (21 Nov 1791-24 Feb 1863) and Nancy Holmes Taylor. Elizabeth Ingram remembered she was calm and steady and always wore a smile. She made delicious biscuits on a big tray. Elvie Hayes remembers her grandmother Cumi said she was not strong. Cumi as a girl intended not to marry and to stay home and take care of her mother, but her mother insisted that she marry.

Jesse Taylor was born in New Bern, North Carolina. He settled in Talbot County, Georgia until 1836. In the fall of 1846, after the Indians had been deported, he moved to the Chewacla Creek area where he built a house in 1854 which still stands about two miles south of the Mt. Olive Church. He is thought to have given the land for the original church. He was one of the original members of the Mt. Olive Church and became a deacon of the church. "He was a quiet unobtrusive man of strong convictions, and though of limited early educational advantages, was qualified to draw clear conclusions from obscure premises, and acted upon them as the rule of his life, respecting the opinions of others, yet claiming the prerogative of cherishing his own." His children were:

1. Francis M. Taylor, built on Odom Creek.
2. Mary E. Taylor.
3. Euphema, who married Maj.E.S. Parks.
4. David J. Taylor.
5. Nancy J., married William Fincher.

6. **Louise C., married Jasper Cooper.**
7. **Mrs. Ivy Cadenhead.**

The Pucketts are buried in the Mt. Olive Cemetery. John Mitchell fought for the Confederacy. At the outset of the fighting, he was too young to go to war but knew he would be required to fight later. Therefore he enlisted at the beginning of hostilities so he could be with his friends. He was wounded in the Battle of Chancellorsville on 3 May 1863 and died in Richmond, Virginia about two weeks later. Jesse Mitchell was visiting his sisters in Shelby County when he became ill and died. He is buried in the Columbiana Cemetery. Gira G. Mitchell established a prosperous country store and probably also owned other businesses in Lee County. He owned several thousand acres of land at the time of his death. He is buried at the Mt. Olive Church. The Moores moved to Shelby County. Virginia and Naomi Key were sisters and descendants of Francis Scott Key, author of the Star Spangled Banner.

Chapter 10

WILLIAM EVERETTE FINLEY

33172 William Everette Finley (7 May 1877-13 Dec 1962)
m 20 Nov 1904 Nora Clemantine Wingard (9 May 1887-14 Oct 1972)
d David Samuel and Nancy Lambert Wingard
lived Shelby and Talladega Cos., AL; bur Columbiana Cemetery

> **331720.1 Atha <u>Pearl</u> Finley (8 Sep 1905-15 Aug 1958)**
> m 10 Dec 1926 Joseph Winters Johnson (11 Dec 1896-   5 Jan 1942)
> he bur Cedar Hill Cem, Bessemer, AL; she Elmwood, Birmingham
> **331720.2 Myrtle Finley (2 Jan 1907-19 Mar 1984)**
> m 15 Jun 1924 Malcolm Tyndall
> m 19 Jul 1928 Lewis Harvey Crowell (24 Jan 1906-6 Jan 1947)
> m 17 Oct 1975 Claud A. Schrock
> bur Sheffeld, AL
>> **A Frances <u>Joyce</u> Tyndall (7 Nov 1925-**
>> m Charles Penhorwood

lived Eaton Rapids, MI
    1 Sandra Cheryl (30 Sep 1943-
  m Dean Leeper
    2 Paula Joyce (19 Aug 1949-
  m Leroy Nelson
      a Mathew Leroy Nelson (Nov 1973-
      b Amanda Joyce Nelson (4 May 1978-
    3 Brenda Frances (19 Dec 1955-
  m Brian Camp
      a Benjamin Alan Camp (22 Apr 1978-
    4 Teresa Marie (21 Dec 1959-
    5 Barbara Ann (7 Jun 1961-
B Dorothy <u>Jean</u> Crowell (8 Jun 1930-
m Herbert Evans
lives Sheffield, AL
    1 Lewis Randall Evans (7 Jan 1947-
    2 Richard Herbert Evans (18 Oct 1949-
      a Jeanie Lucille Evans (14 Oct 1969-
      b Tammy Lynn Evans (10 Oct 1970-
      c Mark Timothy Evans (31 Jan 1975-
    3 Russell Evans (5 Jun 1952-
      a Chastity Lynn Evans (22 Mar 1974-
      b Natasha Marie Evans (3 Aug 1978-
    4 Betty Jean Evans (10 Oct 1954-
  m Dan Mosley
      a Danny Ray Mosley (3 Oct 1971-
    5 Michelle Evans (22 Jan 1959-
  m Charles Sledge
      a Charles Andrew Sledge (13 Jun 1978-
    6 Shirley Evans (6 Nov 1962-
    7 Wanda Evans (17 May 1965-
C Lewey Bennet Crowell (27 Jan 1934-
m 7 Oct 1955 Donna Mae Bowman (25 Oct 1937-
lives Kokomo, IN
    1 Debora Eilene Crowell (25 Oct 1957-
  m Lee Mason
      a Brenda Lea Mason (17 May 1977-

  2 Michael Lewis Crowell (23 Mar 1960-
  3 Jeffrey Lee Crowell (11 Aug 1970-
D Lucille Crowell (7 Aug 1936-
m Richard Coffman (1 Nov 1931-25 Apr 1985)
lives North Liberty, IN
  1 Kenneth Martin Coffman (2 Dec 1956-
  m 26 Feb 1977 Shirley Ann Scutchfield (5 Jun 1958-
    a Andrew Bryan Coffman (4 Jun 1979-
    b Thomas Ryan Coffman (7 May 1981-
  2 Colleen Kaye Coffman (13 Oct 1964-
  m Thomas A. Albert
    a Crystal Lynn Albert
    m Steve Hoxton
      1 Michael Hoxton
E Robert David Crowell (26 Jul 1941-)
m Sandra Chard
lived Mishawaka, IN
  1 Daniel Lewis Crowell (13 Sep 1963-
  2 Timothy Leonard Crowell (16 Feb 1966-
F William Joseph Crowell (26 Jul 1941-
m Sue Anne Patrick
lives Birmingham, AL
  1 Stacie Lea Crowell (30 May 1966-
  2 Melissa Anne Crowell (28 Jul 1968-
  3 Ross William Crowell (13 Apr 1971-
331720.3 Mary Lucille Finley (13 Mar 1909-12 Nov 2001)
m 9 Jan 1927 Thomas E. Merrell (29 Dec 1899-30 Oct 1983)
s Richmond Merrell, bur Andalusia Memorial, Andalusia, AL
  A Thomas Everette Merrell (15 May 1928-28 Oct 1981)
  m 10 Mar 1950 Frances Collins (23 Apr 1930-
  bur Andalusia Memorial Cemetery, Andalusia, AL

1 Kathy Frances Merrell (15 Apr 1951-
m 12 Aug 1972 Edward Burk (Buck) Southall
(22 Jul 1946-   lives Austin, TX
  a Shaun Thomas Southall (21 Jan 1980-
2 Tomi Lesa Merrell (18 May 1954-
m 11 Jun 1977 John Mark Wiggins (15 Oct 1955-
lives Memphis, TN
  a Lindsay Meredith Wiggins (27 Nov 1979-
  b Whitney Victoria Wiggins (20 Jul 1981-
3 Connie Lucille Merrell (9 Nov 1963-
m 5 Feb 1983 Curtis Creech
lives Covington Co., AL
  a Vanessa Brooke Creech (21 Apr 1986-
B Mary Marjorie Merrell (20 Sep 1930-
m 8 Nov 1953 William Terry Stringfellow (25 May 1931-
lives Andalusia, AL
  1 William Terry Stringfellow Jr. (9 Apr 1957-
  m 10 Aug 1982 Lisa Snowden (25 Aug 1961-
  lives Andalusia, AL
    a Natalie Claire Stringfellow (13 Mar 1985-
    b Emily Lois Stringfellow (20 Sep 1986-
331720.4 Lila Katherine Finley (5 Apr 1922-)
m May 1940 Edgar Bennett Vardaman (20 Aug 1919-   )
bur Live Oak Cemetery, Selma, AL
  A Charles Bennett Vardaman (4 May 1942-
  m May 1962 Junita Stinson d James Stinson

     m 1973 Joy Bray d Johnny Bray
     lives Mission, TX
       1 Charles B. (Chuck) Vardaman Jr. (11
       Oct 1963-
       m 1980 Terri Coggins, div. 1988
         a Kimberly Odell Vardaman (10 Sep
         1980-
       2 Christopher Dean Vardaman (27 Feb
       1966-
       m 1987 Tammy
       lives Webb, AL
         a Cesale Vardaman (3 May 1988-
       3 Jeffery David Vardaman (30 May 1967-
       m 1988 Petra Siegel
   B John Everett Vardaman (15 Aug 1943-
   m 1964 Linda Lee Moore (17 Aug 1943-, div
   1979
   m 13 Mar 1981 Rebecca J. Sullivan
   lives Merrill, Iowa
       1 John Everett (Rhett) Vardaman Jr. (10
       Nov 1966-
       2 Jennifer Lynn Vardaman (27 Jun 1969-
       m Aug 1983 Mathew Dobbs (3 Apr 1967-
         a Heather Dobbs (16 Apr 1984-
   C Cheryl Kaye Vardaman (27 Oct 1946-
   m Randall Lee Clark (14 Apr 1948-
   lives Cincinnati, OH
       1 Bryan Thomas Clark (13 Feb 1973-
       2 Kristina Marie Clark (14 Aug 1975-

Will Finley, second son of James Taylor
Finley, was born in Lee County, Alabama
southeast of Loachapoka very near the Macon
County line. He probably attended the first
grades at the Beehive School which was located
near their house. We can imagine he played in
Choctofaula Creek which flowed through their
land. The family moved in an oxcart to Shelby
County when Will was about ten years of age.

Will told his children about driving the cattle behind the cart. After settling near Columbiana they carried logs to Wilsonville to have them sawed into lumber. They brought the lumber back to build their house.

When he was a toddler, Will would sometimes go to the kitchen when his mother was not looking and put his fingers into the sugar jar. If his mother came into the room and caught him he would close his eyes, thinking if he could not see her, she could not see him. On one occasion, his mother baked a cake and left the layers sitting on the table to cool before icing. While she was outside the room she heard Will say to his sister, "Oh Annie, this sure is good sweetbread." He of course was eating the cake. It seems Will had a sweet tooth. As a boy, Will would have to milk the cows. He had to go out at night to hunt the calves. While walking in the woods he heard an owl go who-o-o-o. He told on himself that he replied, "This is just little Will Finley going to hunt the calves."

Will married Nora Wingard who lived on the road halfway between Columbiana and Wilsonville. Nora was the second daughter of Sam Wingard, but the first to marry. Liv was the nosey sister in the family and she found Nora's wedding dress in the closet and her ring in a drawer and showed them to sister Florence. The ring was a broad ring and had Will and Nora's initials inside so they knew who was getting married. Sister Frances was a top-notch seamstress and she made Nora's wedding dress. It had a "dropped yoke" pattern. The top was of white satin and sheared all over. The bottom part of the dress was a more common white material. Her "second-day dress" was tan and trimmed in braid. They were married in the living room of Sam Wingard's house in the afternoon. That night they went to church. Florence Williams was eight at the time and remembers that before the wedding she was in the bedroom crying. Her father was choking back his tears and pretending not to care. He told her, "I wouldn't cry after her. If she loves somebody else more than she does us, let her go."

Nora Finley had joined the Missionary Baptist Church at the age of 15. Will did not join any church until after they had children. His parents were Primitive Baptists and he leaned that way but he was a Mason and Primitive Baptists would not allow members to belong to secret orders. Therefore he joined the Dargen Missionary Baptist Church, where he became the music director. Nora, whose family were all Missionary Baptists, began to lean toward Primitive Baptist teachings. She told the story that at midnight one night she was reading the Bible on the back doorsteps by lamplight after the rest of the family was asleep. She read the passage which said to not let family, child, or anything come between you and the church. She felt the scripture was encouraging her to join the Primitive Baptist Church so she joined the Mt. Olive Church where her in laws belonged. This occurred when oldest daughter Pearl was about 15 or 16 years of age. I can remember as a young boy staying with my grandparents. We were preparing to go to church one Sunday when my grandmother said, "Wayne, whatever happens in church today, I don't want you to laugh."

The occasion which she suspected might lead to mirth was a footwashing ceremony.

Will and Nora first lived in a house near Sam Wingard between Columbiana and Wilsonville and it was here Pearl was born. Next they bought a place near the Antioch Church in the Kingdom Community, again close to Sam Wingard's farm. Will decided he did not want to farm and he hauled cordwood for a short time. They then sold their farm and moved to Columbiana where Will ran a brickyard. They lived in a house on the lot where the current Columbiana City Hall now stands. It was in this house that Lucille was born. After about two years they bought a farm at Dargen, over the hill and behind the farm of Bernard Finley. It was at Dargen that the three oldest girls started to school. The schoolteacher, a Mr. Lyons, roomed at their house. Mrs. Nobie Edwards taught in one room of the school and the principal, Mr. Jim Baldwin, taught in the other room. When Myrtle started to school and Lucille was left at home by herself she insisted on going along. She was allowed to go to school to humor her, thinking in a short while she would become tired and stay at home. However she demanded books and homework like the other girls and the result was that Lucille started to school early at the age of five.

Pearl was the oldest but she was small and frail. Myrtle, 16 months younger, was much larger and stronger. One day they had been fighting and Will got some switches and said, "We are going to play turn and burn." The girl on the side next to him would get the licks. Myrtle was able to hold Pearl so she got most of the damage. Before it was over Will almost had to whip Nora also. Nora was always partial to Pearl, perhaps because she was smaller and weaker than Myrtle. At one time Pearl was thought to be wormy. She complained of stomach spasms. The family took cuticura soap and mixed enough copper and turpentine with it to make it soft. They gave this as a pill to Pearl to kill the worms. She never had any more spasms, perhaps in self defense.

The girls walked two or three miles to school. They had to walk a log over a creek sometimes with the water high. Their uncle Bernard had a fence which went through standing water at times. One winter the pond was frozen over with ice and the girls walked across the ice holding to the fence. They fell through the ice and got their feet wet.

Myrtle told of a time she and Pearl were walking home from school and she took off running and Pearl could not keep up with her. Pearl began to cry as they passed a neighbor's house. Mrs. Edwards overheard Pearl say, "I am going to tell Mama on you when we get home. You know my heart is easy broken." Mrs. Edwards never let Pearl forget this. Years later she would ask Pearl if her heart was still easy broken.

Myrtle tells another story that occurred when the girls were young. They would beg their father for a chew of tobacco and one night he cut all of them a small piece. Pearl put hers in her mouth right away and began to chew it. Myrtle hesitated for a few minutes until she thought it was safe and then began to chew hers. The girls soon were sick and Pearl ran out on the porch and lost her supper. Myrtle did the same thing a few minutes later. After they had gone to bed Pearl had to get up and vomit again. Lucille was the smart one. She just sat on her mother's lap and held her tobacco in her hand. When the other girls became sick she never chewed hers.

It seems Myrtle was always getting into trouble and received frequent spankings. On one occasion Agnes Wingard was staying with them and had a big doll. Myrtle took the doll to her playhouse and Agnes told Nora. For this, Nora whipped Myrtle. Later Myrtle was fussing to herself and Nora heard her and whipped her again. Myrtle went out to the cotton patch and cried. A black woman told Nora she would get sick and Nora gave her another spanking.

In July of 1916, Will's farm was flooded when the creek overflowed its banks. Lucille remembers that only the tassels of the corn were sticking out of the water. They lost their crops and the mule died. The hogs took cholera and died. They lost everything that year including the farm. Will took pneumonia and the family was in dire straights. A neighbor gave them tallow from his butchered cows and they used this to cook with. Warren Wingard brought the girls the only Christmas they had that year.

After they lost the farm Will moved to the Sicard Mining Community which was located southwest of Montevallo. He worked as a carpenter for the mines for two years. They kept seven boarders in their four-room house in Sicard. Half the boarders worked in the

143

daytime and half worked at night. All the Finley family slept in one room. On one rainy day the girls were playing cards. Will helped Lucille in the game. Myrtle became mad and threw her cards in the fire. Will wanted to whip her but Nora wouldn't let him.

The Finleys would pick up coal from along the railroad tracks where it had fallen from the train. On one occasion Myrtle had a big lump of coal and couldn't carry it. She couldn't get it on her back and Pearl wouldn't help her. Myrtle was fussing and Will told her to hush, being afraid Mr. Sicard would hear her. "I don't care if the president hears me," Myrtle said. Will whipped her when she got up the hill.

Will then moved to the Kingdom Community where he farmed his father in law's land. After a year or two he saved enough money for a down payment and bought a farm near Shelby. Father in law Sam Wingard cosigned the note for Will. He tried to tell Will how to farm his land, but Will had a mind of his own and did what he pleased. Will was a good farmer and raised a big crop. After a short period of time, Will cashed in an insurance policy and paid off the loan. Sam Wingard was curious as to how Will was able to pay the loan, but Will never told him.

Will Finley was a life-long Republican, one of the few in Shelby County. Once he ran for county tax assessor. Sam Wingard refused to vote for him because Sam was a Democrat. Perhaps there were a few other Democrats in the county because Will was not elected.

Will's farm was located about 1/4 mile west of the road from Columbiana to Shelby and consisted of 65 acres. Sam Wingard told him he could not make a living without raising cotton, but Will was determined to prove him wrong. He raised sorghum, sugar cane, peanuts, corn, velvet beans, and peas but no cotton. He usually had three milk cows, chickens, pigs, and beef. He made a lot of his money peddling vegetables, milk, butter, and eggs. When the farm work was slack he took odd jobs as a carpenter. Behind the garden of the house stood a two seater outhouse. There were several outbuildings, including a barn, blacksmith shop, and corncrib. The outbuildings were unusual in that all had floors off the ground. They had sheet metal around the posts to keep out the rats. Katherine was born here and the family was living here when all the daughters married.

This is the farm I remember when I stayed with my grandparents three summers as a young boy. I remember riding the mules and walking behind Will as he plowed the field, stretching my legs as far as possible trying to step in his footprints. I remember a German Shepard dog named Pete. Pete was always gentle with me but he could be dangerous to strangers. When Will wanted the cows rounded up he would send Pete into the pasture and Pete was known on occasions to snatch the hair from the cows' tails if they did not move fast enough. There were also two mules. Will never owned a tractor.

Katherine remembered going to visit other members of the family every summer. As a girl she was allowed to bring two or three friends home on weekends. They would frequently rob green apples from the trees and eat them all night. By the time she was a teenager her father had a car and would drive her to basketball games and school plays. The first family car was a Chevrolet and later this was traded for a 1934 model black Ford V-8.

The preachers from the Mt. Olive Church frequently spent the night with the Finleys on Saturday night. The family often attended Mt. Olive and Will would leave a bushel of potatoes or perhaps some money on the table in front of the church for the preacher. Nora's favorite song was "Amazing Grace." The minutes of the Mt. Olive Church reveal that members were often "disfellowshipped" (kicked out). The membership dwindled to the point that the church eventually dissolved. After that, Nora attended a Primitive Baptist Church in Sylacauga.

Once the three older girls went to a lawn party at a Mr. Hendrick's house. They had been forbidden to go to the party and were supposed to be somewhere else. At the party they played a game called Flying Dutchman which involved a lot of running. Lucille fell and broke her arm. She was told it was just out of place and they continued to play. When they arrived home that night they did not wake their parents to tell them. The next morning Myrtle told that Lucille had fallen off the board while crossing the ditch. Over a week later Katherine was sick and Myrtle went over a mile to Shelby to fetch the doctor. While he was at the house he also looked at Lucille's arm. He had her carry a bucket of sand in her hand for some period of time after that, serving as traction to straighten her arm.

One summer the girls attended a 20 day singing school which was held at the Antioch Church in the Kingdom Community. The girls drove the wagon to the school and picked up a wagon load of neighborhood children on the way. They were told if it rained they could stay with friends near the church. The entire schooltime passed and there was no rain. Finally near the end of the school there was a little shower at the church but there was no rain at home. Before the girls could get the mules put away the rain had stopped but they went to different friends homes to spend the night. About dusk Will went looking for them and had to round them and their friends up and take them home. While Will was putting the mule in the barn, Nora wrapped clothes around their bodies under their dresses because she knew Will would wear them out when he got to the house. The next day the girls could not sit down.

One of the favorite family recreations was going to singings. Sometimes Will would be called on to lead. As he walked to the platform the family turned to "Amazing Grace" because they knew that would be the song.

Will served as a substitute mail carrier. He would also drive his car around the countryside peddling fruit and vegetables. For a while he seemed to have boils on his buttocks every Spring. He would have to turn the seat around in the car to hang his bottom off in order to keep from sitting on the boils. Someone advised him to take a teaspoon of salt every morning for 21 days and after this he had no more boils.

Once when Thomas Merrell Jr. and Katherine were on a trip with Will in the car, he stopped and bought a shoat in a croaker sack and put it in the back seat of the car with Tommy and Katherine. Before long the pig was out of the sack and rooting around in the back seat. Tommy said, "This hog is ahogging back here." In just a second he and Katherine were in the front seat with the adults. Will never stopped driving but rode all the way home with the pig loose in the back seat.

Will's determination (stubborness) is illustrated by an occasion when he was returning home and the creek was rising. The water had risen so high the planks had washed off the bridge. He unhitched the mule and had it swim across the creek. Then he returned some planks across the bridge and pushed the wagon across by himself. Then he rehitched the mule to the wagon and continued home.

Tommy Merrell told the following story to demonstrate Will's plainspokeness. He and Tommy had stopped the car to help a friend, Elijah Macon, whose car had broken down. While they were talking a "Russellite" (Jehovah's Witness) lady came asking for donations. Will declined to contribute, but Mr. Macon gave twenty five cents. Apparently she was having the donators sign their name to a list. Mr. Macon asked her to sign his name since his hands were greasy. She asked him how he spelled his first name. Will said,

"You ought to read your Bible and you would know how to spell it."

Will planted just about everything on the farm except cotton. One year he allowed Lucille and Nora enough ground to make a bale of cotton. He broke the ground and plowed it but they had to do the planting and picking. With the money they made from this cotton they bought a living room suit from Sears Roebuck, part of which is in my possession at the present time. This occurred after Pearl and Myrtle had married and Lucille was a teenager.

Will was known for his frugality. At one time Nora grew chickens for extra income. Will would plant rape and vetch for chicken feed, but he would make Nora pay for the seed out of her "chicken money." Nora paid for all of Katherine's clothes, books, and school money out of her chicken money. Electric power was brought to the farm about 1930 and not long after the family bought a refrigerator. Will refused to buy a radio when Katherine was a girl. In later life he had a radio and would listen to the news but then would turn it off. He would not allow Katherine to listen to other programs in order to save on the power bill. One of Will's favorite pastimes was to read the newspaper from cover to cover.

In November of 1944, Will sold the farm and bought eight acres of land about four miles south of Talladega on US 231 in Talladega County. He apparently moved there to be close to Tommy Merrell who lived nearby. He had a pasture where he kept a mule and Tommy's horse. He had a large garden from which he sold vegetables and was also well known for his strawberry patch. One day a man came by and wanted to buy cabbages. Will had big pretty cabbages in his garden. When Will asked how much the man wanted he asked for three or four dollars worth. Will told him, "You can't use that much. You had better take about a dollars worth." He then nearly filled up the man's car with cabbages and charged him one dollar. Tommy was sure Will could charged the man three or four dollars for the same amount of cabbage. Tommy told this story to demonstrate Will's honesty.

Everette Vardaman often tells the story of riding to town with his grandfather when Will was an old man. Two cars had stopped at a traffic light which had recently been installed. Will swung around the two cars and was fussing about people stopping in the middle of the road. Everette said, "Grandaddy, you ran a red light." Will said, "Well when did they put a red light there?" Looking around at the first light he ran a second light. One day when Will was driving home from church he was nearly hit by a train. After that he parked his truck and never drove again.

Will remained active well into his later years. Besides his garden, he worked part-time as a carpenter for Mr. Hyde who owned the Purifoy Hotel and a nursery in Talladega. At the age of 79, Will was on a ladder when he lost consciousness and fell to the ground. In the fall he broke some ribs. It is my impression he suffered a myocardial infarction which was the cause of the fall. However Lucille Merrell does not remember him having any trouble with his heart and feels he only fell and broke his ribs. In any case he never worked again after this time. I am sure after this time he suffered symptoms of congestive heart failure which he had for the remainder of his life. At times he refused to take his medicine and I remember my grandmother saying she put his digitalis into his coffee in the morning to be sure he took it. A year or two before his death, I remember talking to him and was amazed to discover he was mowing his own yard. He was using an unpowered push mower which had been discarded by my mother. When I expressed surprise he was able to mow the yard, he stated he would cut one row of grass down the slope and then pull the mower back to the house and sit on the steps until he could get his breath. This was repeated until he had finished mowing the yard.

During his hospitalization mentioned above, Will was jolly and friendly with the nurses. One nurse said, "Isn't he the cutest thing? His eyes are just beautiful." When Nora heard about this it made her mad. She said, "He didn't have no business up there, he wasn't sick anyway." One day one of the nurses leaned over and kissed him on the forehead just before leaving the room. Tommy Merrell was present and said, "She didn't kiss me!" Will replied, "You don't look as well as me."

His health deteriorated and he was hospitalized for about a month prior to his death from congestive heart failure. The doctor also said he had carcinoma of the prostate at the time of his death. Lucille Merrell sat with him the night before his death. He was delirious all night and told of childhood stories of driving the cattle from

Lee County to Shelby County. He was buried in the Finley plot of the Columbiana Cemetery at the feet of his father as he had requested.

Nora Finley was the second daughter of Sam Wingard. She was not very well educated. Her mother always seemed to be pregnant or else recovering from a miscarriage. Her father asked her to take care of her mother and the household chores and allow older sister Frances and the other children to go to school. He promised her that later he would see she had a chance to become better educated, but that chance never came. She never seemed to mind her lack of education. She believed in hard work and an education did not seem to be important for the work a farm housewife performed. Times of sitting in the house were usually occupied with shelling peas, churning butter, etc. She was an excellent cook. She cooked on a wood stove which had a warming closet on top.

In her middle age she raised chickens in long chicken houses. This was called her chicken farm and she did all the ordering, paying bills, selling eggs, etc. herself. She bought 1,000 baby chicks at a time. When the roosters could be identified in about six weeks, they were sold to pay the feed bill. The eggs from the hens were sold to a truck which came twice a week from Birmingham.

She ordered all her garden and flower seeds from Hastings. She never let anything go to waste. In her old age she visited my house in Abbeville. When a neighbor had more plums than she could use, Nora worked my reluctant wife to make many jars of plum jelly.

After Will died Nora sold the farm in Talladega and lived with Lucille Merrell, who by this time had moved back to Shelby County. About the last five years of her life she lived with Katherine Vardaman in Selma, Alabama. She is buried beside her husband in the Columbiana Cemetery.

After Myrtle married Lewis Crowell, they moved to Sheffield, Alabama where they lived when I was a boy. Some years after Lewis died of an accidental electrocution, the family moved to South Bend, Indiana. All the children still live in that area except Billy, who now lives in Birmingham, Alabama.

Tommy Merrell was raised on a farm on Spring Creek, a tributary of the Coosa River in Shelby County. Some of this land is now covered by the backwater of the Lay Dam of the Coosa River. After Tommy and Lucille married, they moved to Wetumpka where Tommy helped build the Jordan Dam. Tommy followed the construction trade and moved around for a few years, finally settling down in Talladega where he worked as a carpenter for the Bemis Brothers Bag Company. For a while the Merrells owned a country store. They did a little farming, milked two cows, and sold milk and butter. Tommy worked with the Boy Scouts and carried them on camping trips. He loved baseball and attended all the games of the local Bemiston Class D team. After retirement, the Merrells moved back to the family farm where they lived on the shores of Lay Lake. A few years ago they moved to Andalusia to live near their children and they are buried there.

Katherine married Ben Vardaman the night after she finished high school. Ben worked with a road building crew and they moved from job to job in Georgia and Uniontown, Alabama. Ben then went to work for the powder plant in Childersburg and later served in the armed services during WW II. After the war they settled in Selma. Kat retired from the county welfare office as the assistant manager. She still has her father's old blue-back speller and her grandfather Sam Wingard's old sacred harp songbook.

Chapter 11

JOE AND PEARL FINLEY JOHNSON

331720.1 Atha <u>Pearl</u> Finley (8 Sep 1905-15 Aug 1958)
m 10 Dec 1926 Joseph Winters Johnson (11 Dec 1896-5 Jan 1942)
s Burton Henry and Willie S. Thompson Johnson
he bur Cedar Hill Cemetery, Bessemer, AL; she Elmwood, Birmingham
  A Robert Carlton Johnson (23 May 1930-
  m Marion Jeanette Grace Gray (24 Aug 1929-6 Jun 1998)
  lives Phoenix, AZ
    1 Steve Gray (21 May 1950-
    m Marlene
      a Geoffrey Allen Gray (30 May 1975-
    2 Dena Ann Johnson (12 Mar 1960-
    m John Rohrbach
    3 Jeri Lynn Johnson (23 Dec 1961-
  B Joseph <u>Wayne</u> Johnson (16 Apr 1935-
  m 20 Jun 1958 Onie <u>Lenora</u> Faulk (21 Sep 1937-
  d Onie Lafayette and Willie Frank Campbell Faulk

   lives Andalusia, AL
      1 Leslie <u>Suzanne</u> Johnson (20 Jan 1964-
      m 17 Apr 1999 Samuel <u>David</u> Simmons (23
      Feb 1958-
      lives Andalusia, AL
      2 <u>Ken</u>drick Wayne Johnson (25 Mar 1967-
      m 25 Nov 2000 MaryAnn Rabren
      d Bill and Frances Terry Rabren
      3 Brooks Thomas Johnson (8 Nov 1969-

Joe Johnson was the first child born after the
Johnson family moved to Bessemer. There is
some confusion as to the date of his birth.
His tombstone as well as his death certificate
give the date as 1897. The 1900 census which
was taken when he was a child says 1896. I
remember my mother saying he was nine years
older than she. If he were born in 1897, he
would have been less than eight years older.
If 1896 is correct he was a few months less
than nine years older. I also notice on the
death certificate his age was first typed in
as 45 years at the time of his death. Someone
apparently noticed the discrepancy and later
marked through the 45 and wrote in 44 as his
age. I believe in her grief my mother became
confused and gave the wrong year but gave his
age as 45 which was accurate. Joe probably
attended Arlington School, where he received
about a ninth grade education.

Joe is remembered by all who knew him as being
very neat and always well dressed. He usually
wore a suit with a vest and white shirt and
tie. I can remember my grandfather saying
when they were going somewhere, it might take
Joe a long time to get ready. But when he
came out the door everything was in place and
he never had to go back to get his

handkerchief. (I take this story to be an indication that Joe had an obsessive-compulsive nature.) He was a short, thin man. He was dark complected with dark brown eyes and dark hair. He combed his hair straight back and it was liberally sprinkled with gray at the time of his death. He had a bald spot on the back of his head and his hairline was receding.

He loved to fish and hunt. Tommy Merrell told of hunting quail with him. They did not hunt with dogs but would just walk up the birds. Tommy said Joe would walk him down and he would have to rest, but Joe was still ready to hunt. They used to fish together on Spring Creek in Shelby County where Tommy had grown up. On one occasion Joe broke the oar of the boat pushing against a stump on the bottom of the creek. Uncle Tommy later sawed off the handle of the oar to make a paddle. He gave this paddle to me as a memento of my father.

Joe and Pearl were married in the home of the Rev. E. S. Gable. Pearl had moved to Bessemer to live with her aunt Florence Williams while she looked for work. She was introduced to Joe by Myrtle Gilmore Banks, who still lives in Bessemer. After marriage they lived for several months with his family. On 16 July 1927 they bought a house on a 110 by 200 foot lot in the Tennessee farm area, better known as Eastern Valley, for $3,500. The house was located on the corner of Potter Avenue and 7th Street, one block from the main Eastern Valley Road. Pearl had grape vines, fruit trees, and a vegetable garden and she planted pecan trees which still produce nuts. It was in this house I was born. I have been back to see the house and it is in amazingly good condition. The porch that was formerly on the front of the house has been enclosed.

Bob Johnson tells the following story which he remembers from his childhood. "I must have been about eight or nine years old. I had a BB gun but no BB's for it. However I had a small ball bearing, I think it was from a roller skate wheel, which was about the same size as a BB. I asked Dad if I could shoot the ball bearing in the BB gun and he told me no. Later while outside playing, I had to try and shoot the ball bearing in the gun. Of course it was a little too large and got hung in the barrel of the gun. Dad, when he found out about it, proceeded to whip my rear with a hairbrush. After a few licks the handle broke off the hairbrush, but this did not slow him down much. He then used his hand to continue the whipping. His hand hurt much worse than the brush. I have never, ever, even thought of shooting a ball bearing out of a BB gun since." This must have been one of the few times my father spanked either one of us. I do not personally have any memory of ever being spanked or whipped by my father. I remember only one time when he raised his voice. This occurred after I had thrown a rock across the street, narrowly missing a passing car. Katherine Vardaman says Joe never raised his voice. When we were toddlers, he never spanked us or told us no. He would move objects out of our way or get us interested in something else.

Joe worked as a timekeeper for the Woodward Iron Company. James R. Bennett in <u>Old Tannehill</u> says "Woodward furnaces, between

Birmingham and Bessemer, were the nation's largest independent and completely integrated manufacturer of merchant pig iron at the beginning of World Was II." By integrated he meant it "mined its own coal, ore, and limestone and hauled them over its own railroad." Will Finley always considered Joe to be a very smart fellow - probably because he worked with a pencil rather than doing manual work. He appears to have been a very valued office worker. During the depression men were laid off in the office until only Joe and his boss, a Mr. Richburg, were still working. During this period of time most men were out of work or perhaps worked one or two days a week. Joe helped support his mother by helping to make house payments. He also bought coal for the winter for his mother. Pearl had luxuries which most women of the time did not have. Betty Burgin loved to go to Pearl's house because she had an electric stove complete with an oven and an electric washing machine.

Storm clouds soon began to arise. On 10 Feb 1928 Pearl gave birth to a stillborn son. She had "uremic poisoning," or what today would be called eclampsia or toxemia of pregnancy. She had repeated convulsions and nearly died. She had to be admitted to the hospital and was kept there for several weeks. Florence Williams said it was after this that Joe began to drink heavily. His drinking progressively became worse and he began to lose time from work. Sometimes he would miss as much as a week at a time. Myrtle Crowell remembered one time when he was missing Pearl made up the payroll for him. She remembered they took the payroll to the plant where the men were restless, having to wait outside in the rain. Of course Joe eventually lost his job. Mr. Richburg said he was the best employee he had ever had. There was only one thing wrong with him and it was his drinking. (Joe's ability as a valued timekeeper is another indication that he had an obsessive-compulsive nature.) The Johnsons lost their house after paying the mortgage down to about $1,700.

They moved to the Inglenook section of Birmingham where they lived at three different locations, the last one at 3912 39th Court. My earliest memories are of this house, which was a duplex. Joe worked at odd jobs with the WPA. Pearl used her precious appliances to help support the family. Most people at the time did not have ovens or electric washers. She baked pies in her oven and sold them. She also took in washing. Tom Weldon, brother in law of Uncle Tommy Merrell, lived in the same neighborhood. He told of seeing Bob and me delivering the washing to neighbor's houses in a wagon. In 1941, the family moved to a federal housing project called Central City in downtown Birmingham, living at 2508 5th Terrace North. Joe eventually got another job as a timekeeper with National Bridge Company. He gave up drinking but his health remained poor. Florence Williams said his stomach had eaten him up. He made a profession of faith and was baptized into the church. A short time later he made an appointment to see a psychiatrist in the Medical Arts Building at Five Points South. The office was on the seventh floor of the building. Joe and Pearl had registered and were waiting in the waiting room when Joe excused himself to go to the bathroom. Inside the bathroom, he locked the door and jumped from the window, ending his life.

In reflecting on stories of my father, I believe he must have suffered from mental depression. To the best of my memory he was what might be described as a quiet drinker. I do not remember him ever being drunk at home or having alcohol in the house. I do not remember any loud arguments at home. It is my impression when he was drinking, he would take his paycheck, which he would receive on Friday and would not come home until the money was spent. My mother suspected he was sometimes robbed of his money before he drank it all up. In any case he made a sincere effort in later years to stop drinking. I do not know but I feel he joined the church hoping a religious conversion would take away the desire for alcohol. When this did not happen, I assume he became more depressed. He probably realized he could not afford the psychiatric care he was seeking and perhaps did not have any faith it would help anyway. He could not turn for help to an organization such as Alcoholics Anonymous, which was just beginning to be organized about the time of his death. Joe was buried in the Johnson family plot in Cedar Hill Cemetery in Bessemer.

Pearl Finley Johnson was born in Shelby County, Alabama. She was the oldest daughter of Will and Nora Wingard Finley. She began school at the Dargen School, a two-room school about three miles north of Calera. Later she attended schools at Sicard and at Shelby, going as far as she could at Shelby, which was the eighth or ninth grade. There were no school buses at the time so she was unable to go to the high school at Columbiana. There was plenty of work on the farm but it did not pay anything so Pearl moved as a young lady to Bessemer to work, living with her aunt Florence Williams. There she met and married Joe. Her childhood pictures show her as smaller than younger sister Myrtle with extremely light blond hair. As an adult she was short, barely reaching five feet in height. She was plump, weighing about 120 to 125 pounds. As an adult she had gray hair but died it an auburn color. I think of her as like a bantam chicken, small but feisty when mad.

When Joe died, she was left in a destitute condition, poorly educated with no marketable skills and with two small boys. She went to work almost immediately at a small candy store, making a dollar a day to the best of my memory. Within a few weeks she found a slightly better paying job at the Try-Me Bottling Company, which was located on 6th Avenue and 9th Street North in Birmingham. During this period of time I remember such economies as buying "day old" bread from the bakery that had been returned from the stores. It was said to be a day old but sometimes it had mold on it. This was no trouble as we just pinched off the mold spots and used the bread to make our sandwiches. We moved from a first floor apartment at 2508 5th Terrace across to 2509 to a third floor apartment since it was cheaper. During World War II Pearl worked at Rheems Manufacturing Company which made ammunition for the war effort. The Rheems facilities were later occupied by Hayes Manufacturing Company, being located at the Birmingham airport. She undoubtedly made better money there, but she worked long hours. It seems she worked twelve hour shifts, six and I believe sometimes seven days a week. After the war was over, Rheems closed and she worked again for the Try-Me Company. At the time of her death she had worked several years as the manager of the Ace Reweaving Store located on the north side of 4th Avenue North between 21st and 22nd Streets. The business was owned by a Mr. Burch who also owned a tailor business on the corner of 22nd Street and 4th Avenue. At the time of her death she was making less than two hundred dollars per month.

After several years of single life, she married Ferrell Marler. I was not aware of it at the time, but I feel sure she married him for economic security. After a few months he was laid off from his work at the steel mills and refused to look for another job. Pearl wound up supporting him so she divorced him after about a year of marriage. Within a year or two she married Clinton Starnes. Clinton was a hard working man, drawing a pension from the army and working at the Birmingham Housing Authority and as a security guard for Liberty National Life Insurance Company. I believe he had been married for a short time early in life but he had been single for many years prior to their marriage. He provided financial security but the marriage was very unhappy for all concerned and was characterized by constant bickering and arguing. After several years they were divorced about a year prior to Pearl's death.

I think the words that best describe Pearl is hard working. Although she had no skills that paid well, she was very talented at working with her hands in many ways. The last several years she worked as a reweaver, mending clothes so cigarette burns or tears would not be visible. She often did reweaving jobs on the side at night. She also could alter clothes, upholster furniture, and make clothes as well. She rose early, worked long hours, and moonlighted at night. When I was a teenager she made most of my shirts from flour sacks. Although I was often embarrassed by the economies we had to endure, I remember I was not even embarrassed to wear the homemade shirts because they looked as good as store-bought ones. Her most enjoyable leisure activity was going to all-night gospel singings. (The singings lasted all night, but she never stayed that long, usually going home about midnight.) She participated enthusiastically and in fact I can remember how embarrassed I was because it seemed to me that she sang too loud with a piercing, high pitched voice. At times she would direct a song at the singings.

She was one who could do the most disagreeable job without complaining. For instance she was the one in the family who cleaned and dressed the wounds of her sister in law, Laura, whose cancer had ulcerated and drained and smelled bad. I can remember many times when she took control to perform hard tasks.

I have memories of my mother taking me to church when I was a small boy. After Joe died and she had to work such long hours, she dropped out of church attendance for several years. Later in life she became active in church again, joining the South Park Baptist Church on the western side of Birmingham. She became the director of the Women's Missionary Union organization of the church.

She was always in good health. I do not remember her ever missing a day of work due to illness. About the last week of May of 1958 she developed symptoms of congestive heart failure. She turned out to have a pericardial effusion which was causing the heart failure. She rapidly became worse and died on 15 August 1958. The cause of death was suspected, but not proved until an autopsy, which showed an adenocarcinoma of the rectosigmoid colon. The cancer had metastasized widely to the pericardium, brain, and many other body organs. She is buried in Elmwood Cemetery in Birmingham.

Bob Johnson started the first grade at McAdory School on Eastern Valley Road. He later attended schools in Bessemer and Inglenook before finishing Powell Elementary and Phillips High School in Birmingham in 1948. He worked as an usher at the Alabama Theater during school days. He worked at a bakery for several months after graduation. Then he enlisted in the Air Force and retired after twenty-six years of service. He served at several different locations including Knoxville and Johnson City in Tennessee, Fayetteville, North Carolina, Korea, and Phoenix, Arizona. It was while stationed at Knoxville he met Marion. His last tour of duty was in Phoenix and after retirement he settled there. He retired from the welfare department in Arizona in 1993.

As a boy Bob was short and small for his age but I always thought of him as being one of the toughest boys in the neighborhood. As a boy he was chosen for the Pony League All Star baseball team. He was the smallest member of the team by far. They went out of town, I believe to Chattanooga, Tennessee to play a team there. I did not see the game but I was told about it. Bob did not start the game and his team was being beaten badly. In the last inning the coach sent him up to pinch hit. When the other team saw how little he was, they drew all the outfielders in close. Bob then knocked the ball over the left-fielder's head. I remember Bob being chosen by his teammates to bat cleanup in neighborhood games. I was much impressed since I was never chosen for such an honor.

In contrast to Bob, Wayne Johnson attended only two public schools. He finished at Powell Elementary School in 1948, Phillips High School in 1952, Howard College (now Samford U.) in 1956 with an AB degree, and the University of Alabama-Birmingham in 1960 with an MD degree. He was elected president of the student government at Howard. He interned at Lloyd Noland Hospital in Fairfield and had one year of surgery residency at Carraway Methodist Hospital in Birmingham. After practicing for a short time at Pinson in the Birmingham area, he moved to Abbeville, Alabama where he practiced medicine from 1964 to 1968. He then moved to Andalusia where he had a family practice until 1989, then emergency medicine at Andalusia Hospital and several other locations. He now practices family medicine at a rural health clinic in Red Level, Alabama.

He is an active member of the First Baptist Church of Andalusia, serving as a deacon and Sunday School teacher. He served on both the state and Southern Baptist Convention Committees on Commissions and Boards. He also served on the Board of Trustees of the Alabama Baptist Children's Home for thirteen years. He took three short medical mission trips to Honduras in 1972, the Phillipines in 1974, and Guatemala in 1976.

Lenora Faulk Johnson considers the Wicksburg area of Houston County, Alabama as home. Her mother died of cancer of the jaw (it was probably osteomyelitis of the jaw, at least according to her death certificate) when Lenora was about fourteen years of age. Her father was unable to care for her and she lived with several aunts and uncles as a girl. She attended thirteen different schools before graduating from Dothan High School. She enrolled in Howard College in 1957 and attended the First Baptist Church of Birmingham, where she met Wayne. They married in Dothan in 1958. Lenora is an active member of the First Baptist Church of Andalusia where she is a Sunday School teacher, Church Training leader, and has been Mission Committee Director and member of many other committees. She has also served on the Alabama Baptist Christian Life Commission and the Committee on Commissions and Boards.

At this point I would like to reminisce about changes in our world since I was a boy. The first to come to mind is the invention of the refrigerator. When I was a boy we had ice boxes. These required a block of ice which was inserted daily and thus kept food cool.

This meant an ice truck came through the community every day to sell ice. A great treat on a hot summer day was to follow the ice truck as it made its rounds. When the large blocks were cut into smaller blocks, slivers of ice were scattered around the back of the truck. We boys would grab these chunks of ice and suck on them for cooling relief and for slaking our thirst.

I remember as a child lying on the floor to listen to Fibber Magee and Molly, Amos and Andy, and the Grand Ole Opry on a large cabinet radio. We had a phonograph with a turntable which was turned by hand. You could make the music go faster or slower by varying the speed of turning. I well remember the first TV in our neighborhood when I was a teenager. All the neighbors visited the Smiths who owned the set to look at the round nine inch screen. The picture was snowy and there were static noises along with the sound.

Probably the most significant change during my lifetime is in the matter of race relations. When I was a young man there was complete segregation of the races. There were white schools and there were black schools. Blacks could not use white rest rooms, water fountains, restaurants, etc. Service stations had a white men's and a white women's restroom and in the back a black restroom. The black room was invariably much dirtier than those for whites. If a black wanted something to eat from a white restaurant he would go to the back door and wait outside while the food was prepared. Blacks had to live in segregated neighborhoods called Negro or more likely nigger quarters. I was taught a considerate white called a black man a "colored man" or was careful to pronounce Negro instead of nigger. I considered my grandfather to be kind to blacks and he called them "darkies." He did not use the term in a derogatory way. I lived in Birmingham during some of the most widely publicized race demonstrations and incidents but my life was in no way disrupted. I would not have known about them if I had not seen them on TV or read about them in the papers.

In the field of medicine, sulfa drugs were first used about two years before my birth. Penicillin was first used during World War II when I was a child. Since then the number and quality of antibiotics as well as many other medications have greatly increased. I began practice before medicare or medicaid had been conceived. Few people had health insurance and that covered only hospital charges. Most people paid their bills out of their own pockets. The semi-private room charge was $12 in the Henry County Hospital in Abbeville when I started practice there in 1964. A private room cost $15. I charged $3 to blacks and $4 to whites for an office visit. Obstetric care from start to finish cost $75. There was a Dr. Martin who practiced in Headland who charged $1 for an office visit, $1 more for a penicillin shot, and $3 for a house call. Most doctors at that time were general practitioners. There were a few surgeons, pediatricians, and internal medicine specialists. I had not heard of gastroenterologists, cardiologists, oncologists, vascular surgeons, cardiac surgeons, pediatric surgeons, etc., etc. when I first began practice.

Chapter 12

MORE FACTS ABOUT THE MECKLENBURG COUNTY FINLEYS

Before we conclude our history of our own line of Finleys, we will include more facts and considerations about our Mecklenburg County Finleys which give hints about their wanderings. Most of them have led up blind alleys as far as tracing their ancestors is concerned, but future revelations may help those interested in the family history flesh it out or correct parts of it. Many of these facts suggest that George Finley I as well as the others came to Mecklenburg County from Pennsylvania. James, son of George Finley I, married Nancy Ray in Greene County, Georgia. Her father, Isaac Ray, is first found in Fannett township of Cumberland (Franklin) County, Pennsylvania. In 1771, he bought land on the Middle Fork of Goose Creek near the current Mecklenburg-Union County line from John and Ruth Johnston of Lurgan township of Cumberland County, Pennsylvania.

Thomas Finley I married Elizabeth, probably the daughter of Archibald White of the Rocky River area. Worth Ray in <u>Mecklenburg Signers and Their Neighbors</u> says he married Theodosia White. However, there is a record of a marriage of Thomas Finley to Theodosia White in Washington County, Virginia in 1815 and this may be the marriage Ray knew about. This could not be the Mecklenburg County Thomas Finley who died in 1805. Still his statement led to the revelation that Archibald White had a son named Zenos. Our Thomas Finley named a son Zenious. Zenious is such an uncommon name that there probably is a connection. Thomas also named his first son Archibald, which would fit with the pattern of naming the first son after his paternal grandfather. Wills of the Whites of Rocky River show that they once lived in Cumberland County, Pennsylvania.

Thomas Finley I was close to the Rosses of Cabarrus County, North Carolina. Anthony Ross, who had brothers named Joseph Anthony and George, made a bequest to Jane Finley in his will (Mecklenburg County Wills at the NC Archives) in 1789. Mecklenburg Co. DB 13, pp. 694-6 shows that she was the daughter of Thomas Finley. Also, Joseph Anthony Ross named a daughter Jane Finley Ross, suggesting he may have married a Finley.

Joseph Finley was close to Thomas Finley I. He witnessed the deed of sale from James Finley to Thomas Finley. He also moved to Wilkes (Oglethorpe) County, Georgia where his land adjoined one of Thomas Finley's plots of land. He is the only one of the Mecklenburg County Finleys other than James listed in the 1790 census, living in Lancaster County, South

Carolina with one male over 16, two males under 16 and two females in the household. He married Martha, the daughter of John Kennedy of Lancaster County and lived there just long enough to be counted in the census. Joseph disappears from Oglethorpe County, Georgia about 1798 and may have moved to Blount County, Tennessee, where some of his in laws lived. Since his children were young in 1790, Joseph seems much younger than the other Mecklenburg County Finleys. It is uncertain how he is related. Most likely, he was a younger brother of Thomas.

The wife of James Finley was named Margaret in the deed of sale of the land on Rocky River to Thomas Finley I in 1777. We have the signature of James Finley of 12 Mile Creek on his will in 1806. The similarities of writing convince us he is the same James Finley who signed as the first witness of the wills of David Bradford of Rocky River in 1779 and of Thomas Allison of Fifth Creek in Rowan (Iredell) County, North Carolina in 1780 (both wills in the NC Archives). The writing also suggests that he wrote the wills as well as signed them as the first witness. (It was common for the person writing the will to then sign it as the first witness). It should be noted that there are discrepancies in this theory. Finley is spelled with a lower case f in his own will and the upper case F in the others. He spells the name "Findly" in the Bradford will and "Finley" in the others. This seems strange to us, but people of an earlier day were not as finicky as we about these things. One thing these wills suggest to the author is that the James Finley of 12

Mile Creek and the James Finley of Rocky River were the same person.

James' signature on the Thomas Allison will suggests they were related. James lived 60 or more miles from the Allisons. The fact he traveled so far to write the will and witness it required strong motivation. The length of time for him to arrive may also explain why the will was filed as a noncupative will, even though there is a signature at the bottom of the will. From the handwriting, it appears that James signed the will for Thomas. Thomas had apparently lapsed into a coma or died before the will could be written. The will was also witnessed by Theophilus Simonton and the executors were Adam and Theophilus Allison. All three were grandsons of Theophilus Simonton who died in Rowan County in 1757 (Rowan Co. WB A, p. 146). The first Theophilus Simonton owned land in Lancaster County, Pennsylvania and he was taxed there in 1751. Adam and Theophilus Allison were sons of Andrew Allison of Rowan (Iredell) County and Thomas probably was also. There were five Allison men who moved into Rowan County in the 1750's; Andrew, James, Robert, Thomas (a different Thomas), and John. All but James lived at one time in what now is Iredell County. It is likely all these Allisons were brothers. Lancaster County, Pennsylvania Orphans Court Records PGM XXIV dated 4 Jan 1751 reveal that Andrew Allison came to North Carolina from Lancaster County, Pennsylvania. There was a Thomas Allison of London Brittain township of Chester County, Pennsylvania who died in 1738. He had six sons, five with the same names as the Rowan (Iredell) County Allisons and they were probably his sons. He also had a daughter named Margaret and she may have become the wife of James Finley. We should also keep in mind that James Finley married around 1750 or later and the Allisons had long left Chester County by then. In other words, even if this paragraph is accurate, James Finley of 12 Mile Creek may belong to a different family from that of Charles Finley of Chester County, Pennsylvania.

There was a John P. Finley who lived on Waxhaw Creek in Mecklenburg (Union) County, North Carolina from before 1790 till his death in 1839. he married Martha, the daughter of James Walkup. He was postmaster at Findleysville (see affidavit of James D. Craig, Walter Clark Manuscripts vol. III, NC Archives). The Federal Register says this John Finley was born in Pennsylvania. The James Craig affidavit reveals that he talked to Charles Finley, the son of James Finley of 12 Mile Creek, probably on a regular basis. James worked at the Post Office at Findleysville. It is likely that means he worked for John P. Finley, who owned a country store in which the Post Office was located. That probably means that Charles came by frequently to visit his brother and that John was the son of James Finley of 12 Mile Creek.

Chapter 13

FINLEYS IN EARLY PIEDMONT GEORGIA

The research for this chapter was done in order to find the father of William Finley I. Hopefully other Finley researchers will find it helpful in tracing their ancestors. William Finley first appears in the tax records of Clarke County, Georgia in 1803. He was a carpenter and farmer and lived on Barbers Creek near Watkinsville in present day Oconee County. About 1804 he married Elizabeth Haygood, daughter of Benjamin Haygood. In 1820 he lived in Walton County, 1825-6 in DeKalb County, 1828-34 in Monroe County, and died in Chambers County, Alabama in 1840.

There were three other Finley men who appear in the records of Clarke County between 1800 and 1810; Nicholas, Samuel, and Thomas II. Nicholas and William both lived on Barbers Creek and both were members of the Mars Hill Baptist Church. Samuel Finley lived in the same tax district with Nicholas for two or three years. Superior Court records show that in 1805 Samuel sued William for wages due him for work performed in William's carpentry shop. Part of the payment he received was a note on Nicholas Finley owed to William. Nicholas won land in the 1807 land lottery. Samuel Finley paid taxes on the land Nicholas had won so Nicholas obviously gave Samuel the land to satisfy the note. These facts make it plain that these three Finleys were related. Since they seem to be near the same age they probably were brothers. For two or three years Samuel lived in the same tax district as Thomas so Thomas was probably another brother.

Of these four only Nicholas appears in the 1805 land lottery, having one draw. This means he was at least twenty-one years of age in 1803 and had no children. He registered for the lottery in Wilkes County. In 1802 he paid tax in Capt. Coates district of Wilkes county which included the headwaters of Fishing Creek as well as Beaverdam and Rocky Creeks. This means Nicholas lived near the town of Washington on the west side in 1802-3. From 1808 to 1811, Nicholas lived in Morgan County, Georgia within one and one-half miles of George Finley II (# 4). Herald Stout, apparently based on information supplied by a descendent of Nicholas, has his birthdate as 1778. Based on the dates they first appear in the tax records and assuming they were twenty-one at the time, William I was born in 1782, Thomas II in 1783, and Samuel in 1785.

Information on their friends and in laws brings interesting insights on the ancestry of these Clarke (Oconee) County Finleys. Benjamin Haygood, father in law of William

Finley married in Chatham County, North Carolina in 1777. He was the son of James Haygood, who died in Orange County, North Carolina in 1767. Benjamin moved to Hancock County, Georgia after 1790 and to Clarke County about 1800.

Nicholas Finley married Elizabeth Middleton, daughter of Holland Middleton who died in Hancock County in 1795 (Hancock County DB L, p. 147). The Middletons lived on Shoulderbone Creek which before 1793 was a part of Greene County. The connection to the Haygoods and Middletons caused a close examination of records of Hancock County for the ancestor of our Clarke County Finleys but no Finleys can be found living in Hancock County at the time. Hancock County seems to be a blind alley.

Aaron Grier of Warren County, Georgia had a daughter named Katherine who according to family records married a Samuel Finley. The only Samuel Finley available in the area who could have married Katherine was our Clarke County Samuel. Elizabeth Grier, another daughter of Aaron Grier married John B. Finley. John B. Finley filed a lawsuit in Clarke County in 1816. He does not appear in the tax records of Clarke County but he may have lived there for a short time and he may be another brother of William Finley. Warren County seems to be another blind alley since no Finleys lived there either. No information has been found on Thomas Finley II which gives any clue as to his origins.

Rebecca Finley who married Nathan Hamilton in Clarke County in 1820 was undoubtedly a sister of William Finley. We feel sure of this because in March, 1820, William Finley served as a witness against Nathan Hamilton and Rebecca Finley when the Walton County grand jury charged them with living in adultery. Another probable sister of the Clarke County Finleys was Nancy Finley who was married to Parks Middleton in Morgan County in 1811 by John McCoy. Parks Middleton was a brother in law to Nicholas Finley. Both Parks Middleton and John McCoy lived near Jacks Creek in the northern tip of Morgan County. A third probable sister of the Clarke County Finley men was Priscilla Finley who married Robert Middleton in Clarke County in 1806 (Parks Middleton and Robert Middleton were brothers of Nicholas Finley's wife).

Another avenue of research has been to trace the in-laws of the children of William Finley I. Five of his children married people who can be traced to either Hancock or Warren Counties. These offer no help in deciding the ancestry of William because they were probably friends of the Haygood side of the family. Daughter Mary married William Foster in Monroe County. William Foster was the son of Jessie Foster and the grandson of Kimmey Foster. Kimmey Foster lived in Craven and Onslow Counties of North Carolina in the 1760's. By 1787 he was established on Kettle Creek in the southwestern part of Wilkes County and also owned land on Hardens Creek. He was a neighbor there of James Finley (# 11), Matthew Finley (# 12), and Samuel Finley (# 13) but we can be sure our Clarke County Finleys were not children of these men. Kimme Foster died in Morgan County in 1816.

The following family connections contains the most reliable information found on all the Finley families who lived anywhere near Clarke County who were old enough to be possible ancestors of the Clarke County Finleys. The evidence for some is much stronger than for others. Inevitably some guessing is involved and doubtlessly there may be errors.

1. **GEORGE FINLEY I (b1735-b1794)**
   m? Jane
   A. Robert Finley I (-b1828) (#2.)
   B. John Finley I (-c1829) (#3.)
   C. George Finley II (b1760-b5 Jan 1836) (#4.)
   D. James Finley I (a1760-b 5 Jul 1841) (#5.)

See Chapter 5.

2. **ROBERT FINLEY I (-b1828)**
m 18 Aug 1803 Lucinda Finley, d Thomas Finley I (#6)
   A. George W. Finley
   B. Samuel M. Finley (-1869) nm
   C. Leroy J. Finley
   m 23 Jan 1840 Hannah Woodham in Greene Co., GA
   D. Justice (Elizabeth) Finley
   m 27 Feb 1838 William (Erastus) Bradshaw in Greene Co., GA
   E. Margaret Finley
   m 29 Apr 1852 Henry J. Hailes
       1. Virginia Ann Hailes
       2. Lucinda Jane Hailes
       3. John T.M. Hailes
   F. Ann Finley
   G. James Franklin Finley

When Robert Finley I first moved to Greene County, Georgia he lived in the southwestern section near Richland Creek. In 1795 he witnessed a sale of land located between Richland Creek and the Oconee River from Thomas Harris to Oliver Wylie (Oliver Wylie was previously a neighbor of George Finley I in Mecklenburg County, North Carolina. He acted as the agent for George Finley to collect his Revolutionary War compensation.) By 1796 Robert was living on Fishing Creek in the northern part of Greene County, in the same tax district as the other sons of George Finley I.

Robert seems to be the helper in the family. He served as administrator of the estate of Leroy Finley. He acted as agent for paying taxes for Margaret Finley and for two different Jane Finleys. He served as guardian for Thomas P. Finley. The division of his estate is found in Greene County Ordinary Returns and Divisions of Estates 1837-1842, p. 152. Son Samuel M. Finley's will is found in Greene Co. WB 5, p. 349. Robert Finley had only one draw in the 1805 land lottery suggesting he had no children before he married Lucinda in 1803 so he is not likely the father of the Clarke County Finleys.

3. **JOHN FINLEY I (-c1829)**
    A.? John F. Finley (-b1835)
    m? 7 Jan 1830 Delitha Nations in Campbell (Fulton) Co.
        1.? Jeremiah Finley
    B.? James Finley

m 10 Mar 1831 Martha Yates in Fayette Co., GA

C.? Peggy Finley
m 2 Sep 1824 Joshua Betterton in Fayette Co., GA

D.? Deborah Finley
m 11 Nov 1824 Nathan Betterton in Fayette Co., GA

E.? Mary Finley
m 24 Feb 1831 Henry Betterton in Fayette Co., GA

John Finley I lived in the Fishing Creek area of Greene County as early as 1788. From 1789 to 1793 he paid tax on 150 acres on Fishing Creek. From the descriptions in the tax records this seems to be the same land Robert Finley I owned after 1796, suggesting they were brothers. He continued to live in the same tax district as Robert till 1805, nearer the headwaters of the creek than James Finley I. He almost certainly is the same John Finley who lived in district 20 of Morgan County from 1808 till after 1820, near George Finley II. By 1823 he was in Fayette County and appeared in the tax records through 1829. According to the 1827 land lottery he was a veteran of the Revolution. John Finley I also had only one draw in the 1805 lottery, again suggesting he was not the father of the Clarke County Finleys.

Administration records of Fayette County show John F. Finley died by 1835. <u>Campbell County Annual Returns</u> book B, p. 301 dated 1848 records a return of Benjamin D. Smith, guardian of Jeremiah Finley, orphan of John Finley, deceased. Since John F. Finley is the

only Finley associated with Campbell County he
is likely the father of Jeremiah.

4. GEORGE FINLEY II (b1760-b5 Jan 1836)

See Chapter 6. This George is probably the
father of William Finley I.

5. JAMES FINLEY I (a1760-b5 Jul 1841)
m c1795 Nancy Ray, d Isaac Ray
   A.   Isaac Finley (b1800-   )
   B.   George Finley IV (c1800-   )
   C.   Nelly Finley
   m 12 Jun 1820 Allen Johnson
   D.   James T. Finley (c1810-   )
   E.   Nancy Finley
   m Lewis M. Maxey
   F.   Jane Finley
   m 3 Aug 1830 Jeremiah Maxey
   G.   Oliver P. Finley (c1820-   )
   m 22 Oct 1849 Margaret J. Campbell in
   Oglethorpe Co., GA
   lived at Maxeys in Oglethorpe Co.
   H.   Margaret Finley
   m? 3 Jul 1842 Zacharia Freeman

As noted previously James Finley was a brother
of Robert Finley I and the son of George
Finley I. He lived on Fishing Creek of Greene
County from 1788 to 1841 nearer the mouth of
the creek than Robert. Estate papers of
Greene County list him as a legatee of Isaac
Ray. Isaac Ray had lived first in Cumberland
County, Pennsylvania and then in Mecklenburg
County, North Carolina before he moved to
Greene County after 1790. James Finley was a
Revolutionary veteran according to the 1827

land lottery. Indian depredation claims show
he lived in Irwin County for a short time.
His will is found in Greene County WB F, p.
263.

6. THOMAS FINLEY I (b1754-b29 Oct 1805)
m   Elizabeth? White
m 5 Feb 1801 Margaret Allen (widow of William
Allen)
   A. Jane Finley (c1775-
   m b1790 Charles Gillum s Ezekiel Gillum
   B. Archibald H. Finley
   m 29 Mar 1824 Patsey Hines in Granger Co.,
   TN
   C. John Finley (c1780-a1850)
   lived in Noxubee Co., MS in 1850
   D. Lucinda Finley
   m 18 Aug 1803 Robert Finley I
   E. Ireneous (Rene, <u>Rainey</u>) Finley (c1790-
   m 13 Sep 1810 Nancy Martin in Oglethorpe
   Co., GA
   moved to Jasper Co., GA
      **1.?   Thomas Patterson Finley (13 Jan
      1813-9 Jan 1874)**
      m 4 Feb 1838 Mary Ann McClaine in Butts
      Co., GA
      moved to Chambers Co., AL
   F. Mary Finley
   m   Thomas Ward
   G. Dionia (Nicy) Finley
   m 6 Nov 1818 David Elliott
   H. William C.H. Finley II (c1791-a1850)
   m? 8 Dec 1812 Elizabeth Smith in Oglethorpe
   Co.
   moved to Jasper Co. 1815, Alabama Territory
   1819
   lived Noxubee Co., MS in 1850
   I. Elizabeth Finley

m 12 Nov 1818 William Waggoner
J.   Zenious <u>Leroy</u> Finley (c1792-b1819)
will recorded in Granger Co., TN in 1819
K.   Fidella (Della) Finley (c1798-1860)
m 18 Nov 1818 John Shaw (c1790-1863)
bur McKenzie Cem., Homer, Claiborne Par., LA
   1 John Thomas Shaw (c1819-bMay 1887)
   m 31 Jan 1843 Caroline Culver
   2 Patrick L. Shaw (c1821-15 Jul 1866)
   m Melissa T.
   3 David Alexander Shaw (1 Feb 1823-1 Apr 1866)
   m c1848 Sarah A.
   4 George M. Shaw (c1826-   )
   m Caroline Harvey
   5 Mary E. Shaw (c1829-   )
   m 24 Aug 1853 William W. DeLoach
   6 Seaborn Harris Shaw (1832-   )
   m 1859 Lucy Ann Susan Allison
   7 Susan C. Shaw (c1835-   )
   m 5 Aug 1860 M.O. Shaw
   8 Fidella Harriet Shaw (c1838-   )
   m 22 Aug 1867 A.T. DeLoach
L.   Thomas P. Finley (c1803-
m 9 Nov 1823 Anna Waggoner
?   moved to Scott Co., AR

Thomas Finley I first appears in official records when he served in Capt. Adam Alexander's militia company in 1765. He also served on a petit jury in Mecklenburg County, North Carolina in 1775. In 1777 he bought from James Finley land on Rocky River in what is now Cabarrus County, North Carolina (Mecklenburg DB 7, p. 180). Mecklenburg County DB 13, p. 588 and Cabarrus County DB 2, P. 487 prove he moved first to Wilkes (Oglethorpe) County, Georgia and then to Greene County, Georgia. He lived adjacent to

Joseph Finley in Oglethorpe County and on the Oconee River in Greene County in the same tax district as James Finley I (between Fishing and Harris Creeks). He was closely related to several of the previously mentioned Finleys.

In his book <u>Mecklenburg Signers and Their Neighbors</u> Worth Ray says Thomas Finley married Theodosia White. This seems to refer to a Thomas Finley who married a Theodosia White in Washington County, Virginia in 1815. Obviously it does not refer to our Thomas Finley I, but the information fortunately led to a search of records on the Whites of Mecklenburg County, North Carolina. The will of Archibald White in Cabarrus County, North Carolina, dated 25 Dec 1815, names a son Zenos. Thomas had a son named Zenious. Common practice at the time was to name the first son in a family after the wife's father and Thomas named his first son Archibald. This makes us believe Elizabeth was the daughter of Archibald White and they named at least two of their sons for members of her family.

The sons of Thomas Finley are named in his will (Greene Co. Wills 1796-1806, pp. 88-90), Archibald and John being the oldest and one of the middle sons being William C. Finley. <u>Greene County Estate Records 1816-1822</u>, p. 327 has a list of the heirs of Thomas. One of these heirs is W.C.H. Finley, obviously the same as the William C. Finley of the will. Since he was still living in 1850 he cannot be the William Finley I of Clarke County.

Jane Gillum is not mentioned in estate records of Thomas Finley but she was left a bequest in the will of Anthony Ross of Mecklenburg (Cabarrus) County in 1789. Mecklenburg County DB 13, pp. 694-6 reveals she was the daughter of Thomas Finley and DB 16, p. 159 shows she was married in 1790. We feel she had to be born at least by 1775.

7. JOSEPH FINLEY (-b10 Dec 1805)

m Martha (or Margret) Kennedy d John Kennedy of Lancaster Co., SC

Joseph Finley witnessed the sale of land on Rocky River in Cabarrus County, North Carolina from James Finley to Thomas Finley I in 1777. In 1785 and 1787 he is listed near Thomas Finley I in Wilkes County, Georgia. He was granted 200 acres of land on the North Fork of Little River in what is now Oglethorpe County. This land was adjacent to land owned by Thomas Finley. He apparently did not move in Georgia but county lines shifted and from 1792 to 1795 he lived in Greene County and from 1796 to 1797 he was taxed in Oglethorpe County. It seems he lived in present day Oglethorpe County very near the Greene County line. It seems he moved for a short time back to Lancaster County, South Carolina near his wife's relatives. He is listed there in the 1790 census and his name appears in deeds of Lancaster County. He probably moved to Blount County, Tennessee about 1798. He had a brother in law, Felix Kennedy, who lived there. A Joseph Finley was taxed there as early as 1800. A Joseph Finley of Williamson County, Tennessee sold land in Blount County in 1816 which was adjacent to F. Kennedy (Blount DB 1, p. 418). The 1790 census suggests he had two sons under 16 years of age and one daughter at the time.

Joseph Finley obviously is related to the Fishing Creek Finleys but how is uncertain. He seems younger than Thomas and George I but older than their known children. Most likely he is a younger brother of Thomas Finley I and both were the sons of John Finley of Mecklenburg County, North Carolina.

8. JACOB FINLEY
m 14 Dec 1788 Catherine Riley d Jacob Riley in Orange Co, NC
   A.? Mary Finley
   m 13 Apr 1809 Joshua Moore in Jasper Co., GA
   B.? Susannah Finley
   m 25 Jan 1808 John Moore in Jasper Co., GA
   C.?? William Finley III
   m 17 Nov 1811 Elizabeth Lee in Jasper Co., GA
   D. Riley Finley (21 Sep 1793-12 Jun 1871)
   m 8 Jul 1823 Mary Benson in Jasper Co., GA
   divorced 26 Dec 1826
   m 22 Nov 1827 Catherine Oliver
   m 10 Oct 1833 Margaret Eliza Curry
      1 Mary (? Catherine) Finley (14 Dec 1831-5 Jan 1891)
      m J.D. Dunn of Meriwether Co., GA
      2 Harriett Finley (1833-   )
      3 Amanuel Alexander Finley (9 Apr 1836-18 Dec 1921)
      m 30 Oct 1856 Catherine Johnson
      4 Emiline Finley (1842-   )
      5 John L. Finley (1844-   )
      6 Martha A. M. Finley (1846-   )
      7 Iris Anna F. Finley (1848-   )
      8 Laura M. Finley (1850-   )

E. Alfred Finley (1800-1853)
m 4 Jun 1827 Ruth Howard (1805-a1880) in Jasper Co., GA
    1 James Howard Finley (1828-1902), lived AR
    m Eleanor Elizabeth Harris
    2 Samuel Finley (1830-1863)
    m Mary McSwain
    3 Nancy Finley (1834-1903)
    4 John Riley Finley (1836-1907)
    m 12 Sep 1861 Mary Jane (Polly) Briley
    5 Henry Marshburn Finley (1838-   )
    6 Mary Ann Finley (1840-   )
    7 William Finley (1842-   )
    8 Sarah Elizabeth Finley (1844-   )
F. Ammanuel Finley (c1803-   )
m 4 Jan 1835 Elizabeth McLaughlin in Troup Co., GA
    1 Sudie Finley (1843-   )
    m 1859 A.J. Hinton of Meriwether Co., GA

Jacob Finley paid tax in Wilkes County, Georgia in 1787. From 1793 to 1808 he lived on the South Fork of the Ogeeche River in the southeastern part of Greene County. He won land in Jasper County in the 1807 lottery and moved there by 1809.

Jacob Finley witnessed the sale of land from John Moore to Riley Finley in 1818 (Jasper Co. DB 8, pp. 382-3). In addition his wife's maiden name was Riley so there is no doubt Riley was his son. Riley and Alfred Finley shared ownership of lot 32 of district 18 in Jasper County and they had many land dealings in Newton County in the 1820's including one between themselves (Newton Co. DB A, p. 462) so there is little doubt they are brothers. Riley signed a bond for Ammanuel Finley when

he was appointed guardian of Leander
McGlaughlin in Meriwether County, Georgia.
Also Riley Finley named a son Ammanuel so
Ammanuel Finley is likely another son of
Jacob. The inclusion of William Finley III as
a son of Jacob is more problematic. Uzza
Finley (see #9 John Finley below) lived in
Jasper County at the time and this William may
be his son. If Jacob is the elderly male
living with Riley Finley in the 1830 census of
Jasper County he was born between 1760-1770.
He may be the son of Hugh Finley who lived in
Hillsborough, Orange County, North Carolina as
early as 1771. Hugh lived in the same
district as Jacob's father in law.

9. JOHN FINLEY II (8 Jan 1725-16 Jul 1803)
m   Annie Norris (c1738-28 May 1785) d
Benjamin Norris
   A. Vilinda Finley (14 Sep 1754-   )
m   Theodocia Turk (-b10 Mar 1805)
      1. John Turk
      2. Laban Turk
      3. Theodocius Turk
      4. Mary Turk
      m b1805 William Horton
      5. Nancy Turk
      6. Vilinda Turk
      7. Thomas Turk
   B. Mary Finley (4 May 1757-   )? dy
   **C. Benjamin Norris Finley (c1759-16 Sep
   1825)**
   m 3 Feb 1786 Ann Phillips (19 Jan 1770-10
   Apr 1844)
   moved to Clarke Co., AL
      1. Elizabeth Finley (25 Nov 1786-   )
      m? 8 May 1802 David Buckner in Greene
      Co., GA

2.   **Lindy (Linna) Finley (14 Dec 1788-25 Sep 1838)**

m Cader Worley (- 30 Jul 1840)

   a.   **Ann Norris Worley (20 Dec 1814-17 Nov 1822)**

   b.   **Zachariah Finley Worley (13 Jan 1817-   )**

   c.   **Joseph John Worley (21 Feb 1819-8 Aug 1823)**

   d.   **Charles William Worley (5 Sep 1821-**

   e.   **James Cader Worley (5 Sep 1821-**

   m 8 Apr 1841 Nancy Brashears

   f.   **Sarah Ann Worley (26 Mar 1824-   )**

   g.   **Joseph John Worley (26 Mar 1826-**

3.   **Charles Finley (29 Jan 1790-b1850)**

m 23 Apr 1813 Elizabeth Woodward in Clarke Co., AL

4.   **Zachariah P. Finley (30 Jan 1792-10 Aug 1838)**

m 12 Jun 1817 Rebecca Danzey (-11   Apr 1873)

Zach killed by Mexicans in Angelina Co., Texas

widow m 16 Jan 1846 Isham Medford

   a.   **Elizah Rebecca Fenley (16 Jan 1819-17 Jan 1828)**

   b.   **Harriet Elvira Fenley (24 Jan 1820-14 May 1875)**

   m 14 Jun 1837 George F. Allen

   c.   **William Norris Fenley (27 Oct 1822-27 Mar 1899)**

   m 19 Feb 1850 Adaline Hicks

      1.   **Sam Fenley**

      2.   **Mrs. Clara O'Quinn**

   d.   **Pamela Ann Fenley (17 Jul 1825- Sep 1826)**

   e.   **Zachariah James Fenley (30 Nov 1826-27 Mar 1827**

> f.   Linney Amanda Fenley (22 Jun 1828-6 Mar 1827)
> g.   Charles Richard Fenley (12 Oct 1830-16 Apr 1879
> m   Lou Sanders
> h.   John Morris Fenley (5 Jun 1833-9 Feb 1909)
> m 8 Feb 1860 Jane E. Waters
> i.   Zachariah <u>Robert</u> Fenley (9 Oct 1838-28 Jan 1905
> m 1866 Amy Waters
>> 1.   Mrs. Ernest Scott
>> 2.   Mrs. Buren Scott

5.   Uzza Finley (30 Dec 1794-   )
6.   Harriet Finley (7 Apr 1796-   )
m 9 Jul 1815 Robert Collier
m   John S. Roberts
> a.   John Finley Collier (10 Dec 1822-   )
> b.   Lycurgus L. (or S) Roberts (26 Apr 1830-   )

7.   Mary P. Finley (7 Sep 1798-   )
8.   Benjamin <u>Norris</u> Finley (25 May 1801-1868)
m 29 Apr 1829 Deborah Melisa Davis, niece of Jefferson Davis
9.   Joseph Phillips Finley (25 Nov 1802-
m 13 Jan 1825 Aly Boney Everett (widow)
> a.   Sarah Amanda Finley (11 Dec 1825-
> b.   William James Finley (5 Nov 1827-
> c.   Benjamin Norris Finley

10.   William Finley (22 Nov 1804-   )
m 9 Jul 1829 Parmelia Danzy moved to Copiah Co., MS
11.   John Finley (20 Jan 1806-10 Sep 1864)
m 12 Jul 1833 Elizabeth Jane Nunn (23 Jan 1814-
25 Jul 1891) born Twiggs Co., GA

      a. Mary Eugenia Finley (1834-1835)
      died Stewart Co., GA
      b. George Lafayette Finley (1836-1862)
      died Martin, MS
      c. Margaret Ann Finley (1839-1885)
      died Bowling Green, KY
      d. Edmund Norris Finley (1841-1861)
      died Bowling Green, KY
      e. Sara Almeida Finley (1844-1927)
      died Alvarado, TX
      f. John Hawkins Finley (1847-1919)
      died Estancia, NM
      g. William V. Finley (1850-1924)
      died Santa Anna, CA
      h.   Debbie Turissa Geraldine Finley (1853-1906)
      m 19 Jan 1869 William D. Whitted
      died Estancia, NM
    12. Nancy Finley (24 Aug 1809-   )
  m 7 Jun 1826 Richard Danzey
      a. Richard Jackson Danzey (-13 Aug 1833)
      b. Nancy Danzey
      m 8 Apr 1847 James C. Worley
D. Charles Finley (c1761-1787)
  1. James Finley (c1787-   )
E. Uzzah Finley (1762-   )
m   Milly
moved to Jasper Co., GA, then Izard Co., AR
  1. Nancy Finley (22 Sep 1787-   )
  2. William Finley
  3. Zach Finley
  4. Charles Finley
F. Eleven Finley (29 Apr 1769-23 Dec 1829)
m   Wall, d Arthur Wall
m   Mary (Polly) Taylor (-11 Nov 1839)
moved to Izard, Lawrence Co., AR
  1. Rachel Finley (25 Sep 1795-)
  m   Joseph Ogletree

2. **Rebecca Finley (3 Jul 1797-)**
m 15 May 1815 Alexander Houghton (? Horton)
3. **Issac L. Finley (25 May 1800-24 Aug 1863)**
m Hila Martin
4. **Matilda Finley (22 Sep 1801-1835/40)**
m   James Davis
5. **Elizabeth Finley (2 Nov 1803-1827)**
m   James A. Harris
6. **Nancy Finley (29 Nov 1805-1830)**
m   Richard Harris
7. **Linny (Linsey) Finley (29 Oct 1807-**
m   William Criswell
8. **John Finley (2 Oct 1809-5 Nov 1874)**
m 17 Oct 1839 Rosetta Ann (Rosey) Bowen
9. **Mary Norris Finley (23 Jan 1812-6 Nov 1889)**
m 30 Apr 1835 James A. Meacham
10. **Julia Ann Finley (6 Oct 1815-   )**
m 7 Nov 1833 Napoleon Bonaparte Allen
11. **William Finley (15 Dec 1818-9 Nov 1839)**
G. **Rebekah Finley (c1770-   )**
m   John Dean (1759-13 Jan 1837)
moved to Clarke Co., AL
1. **Nancy Anne Dean**
m   Coleman
2. **Margaret Dean**
m Robert Lee
3. **Jane Pope Dean**
4. **Rebecka Dean**
5. **Linda Dean**
m William R. Hamilton
5. **John Dean**
6. **Nathaniel P. Dean**
H. **William Finley IV (11 Oct 1772-b10 Nov 1822)**
m 29 Jun 1805 Polly Sharpe (-28 Oct 1856)

moved to Morgan Co., GA
widow married William Broughton, moved to
Nacogdoches, TX

1. **John Finley (10 Apr 1806-   )**
2. **Linney Finley (14 Oct 1807-   )**
3. **Nancy Ann Finley (12 Jan 1808-   )**
m 6 Jan 1827 James Towson in Morgan Co.,
GA
4. **Caroline Finley (23 Feb 1810-   )**
5. **Charles Henderson Finley (24 Apr 1812-12 Sep 1864)**
m 27 Oct 1835 Nancy Broughton
moved to Texas

   a. **Mary Sophronia Finley**
m John P. Whitaker
   b. **John Broughton Finley (2 Nov 1838-6 Jun 1916)**
served CSA Co. B, 8th Texas Infantry
   c. **Lucinda Ann Finley (14 Feb 1841-**
m 1866 Valentine Columbus (Joe) Whitaker
     1. **Mary Celestial Whitaker**
m 1886 Frank Sexton Rook (1865-1932)
     2. **Charles Richard (Dick) Whitaker**
     3. **Lucy Whitaker**
   d. **William Henry Finley (6 Mar 1843-6 Jan 1879)**
m 19 Dec 1872 Martha J. Thomas
served CSA Co. B, 3rd Brigade, TX
     1. **William C. Finley**
     2. **John B. Finley (1 Jan 1877-**
     3. **Harriet A. Finley (c1879-**
   e. **Elizabeth Ella Finley (7 Dec 1847-**
   f. **Kizziah Amanda Finley (16 Apr 1850-10 Jan 1923)**
m 24 Jul 1873 Dr. John Whitaker
m 17 Mar 1885 Dr. Washington Irving Coon

bur Douglass Cemetery, Nacodoches Co.,
TX
   1. **Clinton Whitaker** (c1877-
   2. **Lucy B. Whitaker** (c1877-
   3. **Heneretta Whitaker**
  g. **Tyree Anthony Judson Finley** (18 Feb
1853-
  h. **Nettie Finley** (c1855-   )
6. **William Finley** (-b31 Oct 1849)
  a. **George Washington Finley** (25 Sep
1826-   )
  m 19 Jan 1862 Harriet Muckeroy in TX
7. **Keziah Catherine Finley** (1818-15 May
1853)
  m 26 Dec 1850 Bennett Blake in
Nacogdoches, TX
8. **George Finley**
9. **Tyre G. Finley** (3 Aug 1823-   )

Rosemary C. Neal of 23 Terrace Road, Hampton,
VA 23661 has shown that this John Finley was
born in Prince Georges Co., MD, the son of
Charles and Elizabeth Harris Finley. Charles
and Elizabeth married in Prince Georges County
11 Apr 1711 (marriage and birth records are
found in Prince Georges County Church
Registers). Stout says Charles Finley was the
son of Robert Finley who died in Talbot Co.,
MD before 1717. At the time of the Revolution
John Finley lived in 96 District, South
Carolina (Revolutionary pension application of
Uz Finley, # R3557 in the National Archives).
Neal says he lived in current day Newberry
County near various in-laws. He was granted
land in Greene County, Georgia in 1786. He
and his sons lived in the western portion of
Greene County near the confluence of the
Apalachee and Oconee Rivers. Son Charles was
killed by the Indians in the raids of 1787/8.

John Finley's will is found in <u>Greene County Wills 1796-1806</u>, pp. 54-5. Most of the information on the family of Norris Finley comes from a family Bible in the possession of Lleta Lightfoot, P.O. Box 432, Alvarado, TX 76009. She has a letter William Finley of Copiah County, MS sent her ancestor John Finley. Willis T. Finley of 307 Fairview Drive, Longview, TX 75604, a descendant of Eleven Finley, has provided the names of the children of Eleven and Uzziah Finley.

10. JAMES FINLEY II
   A.? William Finley V
   B. Richard Finley (b1782-   )
   m 15 Oct 1815 Matilda Ellenson in Jones Co., GA

The information on this family is perhaps the sketchiest of all in this chapter. There were two James Finleys in Greene County, Georgia listed in the 1805 land lottery, one of them apparently this James. He and son Richard were living in Carlton's District when he won land in the 1807 lottery. He sold this land to son Richard (Jasper Co., GA DB 3, p. 445-6; Jones Co. DB A, p. 417-8). Carlton's is the same district in which lived the sons of John Finley II (#9). I have been unable to find him in the tax lists but son Richard is listed in the same district from 1804 to 1808. This may mean James lived in the town of Greshamville and paid his taxes in town. He lived in Jones County, Georgia from 1808 to 1816. He probably moved to Mississippi with son Richard after 1816.

There were two William Finleys taxed in the same district as John Finley II (#9) in 1799, only one of which could be the son of John. Since James II lived in this district later and we have no idea how long he may have lived there it is entirely possible he was the father of the second William. It is possible this William Finley V is the one in the northern part of Clarke in the 1802 tax list and that he moved across the line into Jackson County where he was taxed from 1803 till 1805. The William Finley of Jackson Co. had 2 draws in the 1805 lottery suggesting he had children before 1803.

11. JAMES FINLEY III (?1760-b6 Nov. 1820)
m Isabella(-b13 Dec 1848)
   A.   Thomas Finley (-c1813)
   B.   Samuel Finley (1790-a6 Sep 1873)
   m 6 Aug 1812 Catherine Greene in Wilkes Co., GA
   will in Chatooga Co., GA WB 1, pp. 75-8
   C. Mary Finley
   m 19 Nov 1818 David Lawson in Wilkes Co.
   D.? Margaret Finley
   m 13 Aug 1818 David Daniel in Wilkes Co.
   E.   Elizabeth Finley
   m 16 Aug 1821 James Lyle
   F.   James Finley (-b7 Sep 1872)
   lived Hillsboro, Union Co., AR
   G.   William Finley VI (a1803-   )
   lived Claiborn, MS in 1836 (Wilkes DB MMM, p. 441)
   H.   John Finley (c1804-c1858)
   I.   David Finley (8 Apr 1813-2 Jan 1858)
   m 7 Apr 1841 Emily W. Goode in Montgomery, AL
   Presbyterian minister in Montgomery, AL

J. Jane Finley
m 19 Nov 1826 Richard Sappington in Wilkes
Co.
K. Isabella Finley (1806-1876)
m 29 Sep 1825 Thomas Greene, Jr. (1800-1864)
buried Matthews Chapel Cemetery, Talbot Co.,
GA
L. Grace Finley
m 20 Dec 1821 Robert Rounsevalle in Greene
Co.
lived Summerville, Chatooga Co., GA

James Finley III lived in Wilkes County as
early as 1778. He fought under Col. Elijah
Clarke in the revolution. He lived on Little
River near Kettle Creek southwest of the town
of Washington. About 1786 he moved to Camden
County, Georgia, returning to Wilkes County by
1791.   He helped build the Hopewell
Presbyterian Church. His son William Finley
VI was a minor as late as 1824 so he could not
be the Clarke County William Finley I. See
below for my belief this James is a brother of
Matthew Finley and the son of Samuel Finley.

12. MATTHEW FINLEY (1758-b Sep 1819)
m Jane McCord
lived Wilkes, Camden, and Oglethorpe Cos., GA
  A. Anna Finley
  m   Smith
  B. Nancy Finley
  m   Walker
  C. Samuel P. Finley (b1800-   )
  m 17 Feb 1817 Sally Mitchell in Oglethorpe
  Co.
  D. Malinda Finley
  E. Polly Finley
  F. Hariot Finley

G.   Jane Finley
H.   John Jefferson Finley (b1810-   )
m 8 Nov 1838 Mary Ann Lane in Newton Co., GA
I.   James M. Finley (a1810-   )
m 25 Feb 1839 Eliza Lane in Newton Co., GA

Matthew Finley was born in Ireland according to <u>Roster of Revolutionary Soldiers in Georgia</u> by McCall but he was in Georgia before the revolution (or possibly in South Carolina - there are Revolutionary War records about him found in the South Carolina archives). I have been unable to locate him between 1780 and 1790. He may have lived in Camden County or maybe South Carolina. After 1793 he was settled on Big Creek in Oglethorpe County, Georgia. In 1790 Matthew was taxed in the same district of Wilkes County as James Finley III (#11) and Samuel Finley (#13). James Finley III and Matthew both lived for a time in Camden County, Georgia. South Carolina revolutionary records reveal a Lieutenant Matthew Finley and a James Finley who on one occasion took Matthew a message. In addition Matthew Finley witnessed a deed in which James III bought land in Wilkes County (Wilkes Co. DB BBB.p. 151) in 1815. These close connections between Matthew and James III suggest that they were brothers since their children were near the same ages. They were probably both sons of Samuel Finley (see # 13 below). Matthew's will is found in Oglethorpe County WB B, p. 171.

13.   SAMUEL FINLEY
   A.?   James Finley III (#11)
   B.?   Matthew Finley (#12)
   C.   Elizabeth Finley (b1774-   )

D. Mary Finley (b1774-   )

From 1785 to 1794 Samuel Finley was taxed for 400 acres of land on Little River in Wilkes County in the same district as James Finley III (#11). In 1792 Samuel, Elizabeth, and Mary Finley sell land to James Finley III (Wilkes DB II, p. 536). In 1793 Samuel Finley sold 200 acres to daughters Elizabeth and Mary Finley (Wilkes DB LL, p. 70). Later Mary Finley sold her land to James Finley III (Wilkes Co. DB RR, p. 324). Obviously all these Finleys were related. The deeds also show Samuel had adult daughters in 1792. The most likely interpretation of these facts is that Samuel was anticipating his death and disposing of his property. He must have been the father of the others. We should also add that two of the older sons of both Matthew (#12) and James were named Samuel. One researcher says one of the grants in Wilkes Co. was to Samuel P. Finley. The printed records I have seen do not have the middle initial. The full name of the son of Matthew was Samuel P. Finley.

14. REV. ROBERT FINLEY (1772-1817)
m 16 May Easter Flint Caldwell (1772-1844)
- A. Helen S. Finley
- B. James C. Finley
- C. Josiah Finley
- D. Robert Finley
- E. Ann Finley
- F. John E.C. Finley
- G. Susan Finley
- H. Hannah Finley
- I. Mary Finley
- m   John R. Davidson

Rev. Robert Finley was a renowned Presbyterian minister from New Jersey. He was appointed president of Franklin College (now the University of Georgia) in Athens. He had been in Georgia only a short time when he died suddenly. His will is located in <u>Clarke County Will Book A</u>, pp. 74-5. His family apparently moved back north after his death.

15. JOHN FINLEY III
m   Margaret

There was a John Finley with wife and three children who immigrated to Georgia from Ireland in 1772. This is the time Wilkes County was being settled. The <u>Ceeded Lands Journal</u> for Wilkes County reveals a Margaret Finley, widow of John Finley was granted 100 acres of land on the Ogeechee River in 1774-5. Since this John Finley was dead in 1775 he could not be the father of the Clarke County Finleys.

16. JAMES FINLEY IV (-b1806)

There was a James Finley (often spelled Finney so this probably was not a Finley at all) taxed for 200 acres of land on Hardens Creek in Wilkes Co. from 1794 to 1805. Hardens Creek is on the other side of Little River from where James (#11) and Samuel Finley (#13) lived. Each year James Patterson acted as his agent in paying his taxes. His orphans had a draw in the 1807 lottery with James Patterson as their guardian. James Patterson paid tax for James Finley, deceased through 1809 and we see no mention of this family after 1809. The estate of James Finney in Wilkes Co. WB 1806-1808 seems to be his. Friends Alexander Harper and James Patterson were executors. He left his entire estate to daughter Sarah McCormick Finney except $50 to Mary Byington. William Malear was appointed guardian of Sarah Finney, orphan of James Finney decd Jul 1811 in Early Records of Georgia, Wilkes Co. Vol. 2, p. 225.

17. Howard Finley

There was a Howard Finley taxed in the Hardens Creek area of Wilkes County in 1791 and 1792. Since James IV appears in this area in 1794 they may be related. Howard Finley is probably the same man of that name who lived in Pendleton District (Pickens County), South Carolina. This is particularly interesting since the Pickens County, South Carolina Finleys had Haygood neighbors and the Finley and Haygood names frequently appear on the same documents. There was even a James Finley who was administrator of the estate of Col. Benjamen Haygood in Pickens County in the 1830's.

There is some suggestion Benjamin Haygood, father in law of our Clarke County William Finley, was related to the Pickens County, South Carolina Haygoods. He had brothers named James and George which are the names of the earliest Pickens County Haygoods. A George Partin witnessed the will of Benjamin's father, James Haygood of Orange County, North Carolina. A Partain Hagwood (Hagwood is a variation of the spelling of Benjamin's name) appears in the estate papers of Simeon Williams of Abbeville District, South Carolina in 1802. Parten "Hagwood" moved to Decatur County, Tennessee where the 1850 census has him born in North Carolina in 1785. These hints plus the fact Nicholas was in Wilkes County, Georgia in 1803 make us desire more information on the family of James Finley IV. All we can say at present is he had children who were still under age in 1806 (born after 1792). Unfortunately I have been unable to trace the origins of either James Finley IV or James Patterson. Howard Finley apparently is the one who moved to Hopkins County, Kentucky. Some of his descendants say he was born in Virginia.

18. AMON FINLEY

There was a carpenter named Amon Finley who had two draws in the 1805 land lottery in Greene County, Georgia. I have seen no other reference to him. Since Jacob Finley had a son named Ammanuel this Amon Finley may be related to Jacob (#8).

1820 Map of Piedmont Georgia showing approximate locations of various Finley families. Where one man appears more than once, he lived at each location at different times. Numbers correspond with the numbers associated with the families in Chapter 13.

W = William Finley; N = Nicholas Finley; S = Samuel Finley; T = Thomas Finley; H = Nathan Hamilton; D = Daniel Stamper; R = Robert Finley II; 9H = William Finley IV (son of 9); 10A = William Finley V (son of 10); 10B = Richard Finley (son of 10)

Chapter 14

JOHN FINLEY AND DANIEL BOONE

History records that John Finley led Daniel
Boone into Kentucky. It was not that people
had been unable to get to Kentucky. Many had
hunted and trapped there and the fertility of
the land was well known to early pioneers.
The problem was that the only way known into
Kentucky at the time was by rafting down the
Ohio River. The way back up the river was so
difficult and dangerous that it was not very
practical to settle there.

There were many John Finleys in America at the
time, so it is not easy to decide which one
led Boone. Many different John Finleys have
been nominated as the one by their respected
descendants. The one who seems to have the
strongest claim is the John who was the son of
Archibald Finley, who died in Bucks County,
Pennsylvania about 1750. According to most
histories, Archibald had immigrated from
County Armagh, Northern Ireland. His will
names one of his executors as his son John

John Finley married Esther Harris, the daughter of John Harris. John Harris owned a trading post and an associated ferry across the Susquehanna River. The settlement that grew up around his store eventually came to be known as Harrisburg, now the Capital of Pennsylvania.

John Finley first met Daniel Boone when both served as teamsters in the ill-fated Braddock campaign to try to take Ft. Duquesne from the French in 1754. They discussed the new land of Kentucky around campfires while on this expedition. Their lives were undoubtedly saved by the young colonel named George Washington. History records that most of the wagons for the Braddock expedition came from Pennsylvania. This fact supports the claims favoring this particular John Finley over others who lived in Virginia or North Carolina.

Afterwards, their paths diverged and Daniel Boone moved to the frontier area of North Carolina. John Finley lived for a few years at Pittsburgh after it had been ceded to England by the French at the end of the French and Indian War and renamed from Ft. Duquesne.

John made several hunting trips into Kentucky during this time and made friends of the Indians. At the completion of one of his trips in 1767, he had lots of furs to transport back to the colonies. He persuaded the Indians to show him an overland route out of Kentucky and back to civilization.

He was in the habit of trading his furs for merchandise and then peddling this on journeys through the colonies. On one of his trips into North Carolina, he chanced to meet Daniel Boone again. Knowing of his interest in Kentucky, he informed him that he had found an overland route into Kentucky. In 1769, they formed an expedition of seven or eight men and took a hunting and trapping trip through the Cumberland Gap into Kentucky. The rest, as they say, is history. Cumberland County, Pennsylvania Deed Book 1C, p. 344, dated in 1772, describes this John Finley as "late of South Carolina", which also supports the idea that he was a peddler who traveled through the southern colonies.

While we are on the subject of Finleys and frontier celebrities, we should mention that Davy Crockett married Polly Finley, the daughter of William Finley. She died before him and he remarried, but Polly was the mother of his children.

BIBLIOGRAPHY

The Alabama Historical Quarterly, Vol. 15, No. 2.

Andrea, Leonardo, Findley-Finley. A genealogical study of the Finleys of South Carolina.

Bingham, Caroline, The Kings and Queens of Scotland.

Culson, Howard McKnight, The Tinkling Spring - the Headwater of Freedom.

Dickinson, William Croft, Scotland From the Earliest Times to 1603.

Ellis, Peter Beresford, MacBeth-High King of Scotland. Barnes and Noble Books, 1980.

Eyre-Todd, George, Highland Clans of Scotland.

Hall, David M., Once upon a Time - a History of Emory Chapel Community. (Chambers Co., AL).

Hanna, Charles A., The Wilderness Trail.

Hanna, Charles A., The Scotch-Irish.

Hunter, C. L., Sketches of Western North Carolina.

Innes, Sir Thomas of Learney, The Tartans of the Clans and Families of Scotland.

James, Marquis, Andrew Jackson, the Border Captain.

Johns, Rev. J. H., A History of the Rock Presbyterian Church in Cecil County, Maryland.

Kirkham, E. Kay, Survey of American Church Records.

Leyburn, James G., The Scotch-Irish, a Social History. The University of North Carolina Press, 1962.

Lindsey Bobby L., The Reason for the Tears, a History of Chambers County, Alabama, 1833-1900.

McCauley, I. H., Historical Sketch of Franklin County, Pennsylvania.

McGee, Thomas D'arcy, A History of the Irish Settlers in North America.

Morris, Aubrey R., The Haygoods of Mars Hill. 1996.

Pancake, John S., This Destructive War - The British Campaign in the Carolinas, 1780-1782. The University of Alabama Press, 1985.

Ray, Worth S., Mecklenburg signers and their Neighbors (The Lost Tribes of North Carolina), part III.

Reid, Frances W. and M. B. Warren, Mars Hill Baptist Church 1799 to 1875, Oconee County, Georgia.

Rice, Dr. T. B. and Carolyn White Williams, History of Greene County, Georgia.

Stout, Herald F., The Clan Finley. The Eagle Press.

Sullivan, Mrs. B. A., History of the Waxhaws.

Thornton-Cook, E., Their Magesties of Scotland.

Tompkins, Daniel Augustus, History of Mecklenburg County and the City of Charlotte.

Wheeler, John H., Reminiscences and Memoirs of North Carolina.

White, Katherine Keogh, The King's Mountain Men.

Wright, John Peavy, Glimpses into the Past From My Grandfather's Trunk.

Rev. William Milton Mitchell

Mary Taylor Mitchell

James Taylor Finley

Cumi Mitchell Finley

James Taylor and Cumi Finley

James Taylor and Cumi Finley sitting with
James Taylor Jr. between them
Mary and Annie Finley on either side, unsure
which is which
Back, l-r, Charles, Will, Bernard, unknown

James and Cumi Finley on their 50th wedding
anniversary with Lucy Mullin on left and Mary
Latham on right
Behind them, l-r, Virgil, Will, Nora, Bernard,
and Essie Finley—Howard Finley is behind Essie
Pearl Finley is in front of Lucy Mullin—other
children, l-r, Maxine, Dewey, Elvie holding
Willie Mae, unknown

Will Finley, Joe Johnson, Katherine Finley,
and James Taylor Finley, l-r

Will Finley

Will Finley holding Pearl and Nora holding
Myrtle

Will and Nora Finley

Pearl, Lucille, and Myrtle Finley, l-r, when
they lived at Sicard

Pearl Finley Johnson

Pearl Johnson holding (?) Wayne

Pearl Johnson holding Bob

Joe Johnson holding Bob

Bob and Wayne Johnson in car with Joe standing
beside it

Bob Johnson

Lewis and Myrtle Crowell with Joyce

Pallbearers at Nora's funeral
Front, l-r, Wayne Johnson, Bob Johnson, Bobby
Crowell, Charles Vardaman
Back, l-r, Lewey Crowell, Tommy Merrell,
Everette Vardaman, Billy Crowell

INDEX

ABOUT THE AUTHOR

The author is a native of Birmingham, Alabama, now lives in Andalusia. He is a Medical Doctor and amateur Genealogist. He has spent the past thirty years researching this book. He has taught several genealogy classes in Andalusia.

www.ingramcontent.com/pod-product-compliance
Lightning Source LLC
Chambersburg PA
CBHW030257290526
45785CB00001B/125